THE
LONDON
MAPGUIDE
Michael Middleditch

P9-BAT-564

CONTENTS

All maps in this Mapguide are based on Aerial Photographs supplied by Aerofilms Ltd.
with an original Ground Survey carried out by MICHAEL GRAHAM Publications.

PENGUIN BOOKS

UNDERGROUND

London Travel Information 020 7222 1234 24 hours
Minicom 020 7918 3015

© London Regional Transport

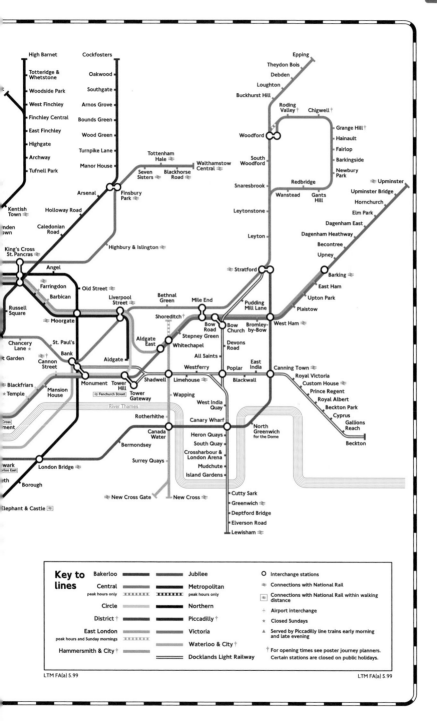

Key to lines

Bakerloo		Jubilee	
Central		Metropolitan	
peak hours only		peak hours only	
Circle		Northern	
District †		Piccadilly †	
East London		Victoria	
peak hours and Sunday mornings		Waterloo & City †	
Hammersmith & City †		Docklands Light Railway	

○ Interchange stations

⇌ Connections with National Rail

▣ Connections with National Rail within walking distance

✦ Airport interchange

★ Closed Sundays

▲ Served by Piccadilly line trains early morning and late evening

† For opening times see poster journey planners. Certain stations are closed on public holidays.

INTRODUCTION AND HISTORY

A RETROSPECT

I was born in London and spent my early life living in a mundane suburb of London, so it was always a great pleasure for me to escape into Central London. My parents must have felt the same for they delighted in walking my brother and me around the city, always stopping at the statues - Edith Cavell (E5 31) was a favourite - and grappling with the history relating to the monuments. At that time London's sky appeared to be full of barrage balloons and there were even sheep in Hyde Park; the avant-garde dance was the 'jitterbug' imported by American G.I.'s; and the streets seemed to be full of soldiers and sailors from all the countries in the world.

Probably the most exciting day trip was to the London Zoo. This was an annual event and I keenly looked forward to our leisurely planned walk around the confines of what was then a rather cruel way of keeping animals; but it was neverthless exciting. We always went as a family to the theatre at least once a year, the Palladium for variety shows, and then after the war to Drury Lane, the Coliseum and the marvellous Stoll Theatre in Kingsway (long since demolished for an office block), where we saw all the great American musicals.

When I reached my 'teens' it was football and cricket and music as well that attracted me to London. I can't believe how many times I saw opera at Covent Garden in a year - prices have gone up! I remember a concert at the Festival Hall sitting behind the massive shoulders of Vaughan Williams. The 100 Club in Oxford Street (which amazingly is still there) and the bebop clubs scattered around Leicester Square were also popular haunts of mine at that time. Another pastime for me was roaming and rummaging through Foyles and the numerous secondhand book and record shops in Charing Cross Road looking for bargains. Most of my early working life was spent working in Fleet Street...I loved it - the cosy little pubs scattered around the area offering bitter and home-made food (pre-microwave), and perhaps even a glimpse of my favourite newspaper cartoonist. The office I worked in was on Fleet Street so we were able to see the Lord Mayor's parade and all the visiting dignitaries. I remember rushing out into the street to see my hero Yuri Gagarin - hardly anybody was there to see him, so my colleague and I got a special wave. In the evenings I walked back to Liverpool Street Station past bomb damage from the war that had not been reconstructed. In later years my steps were quicker as I eagerly looked forward to seeing my wife and our newborn son in the summer months waiting at the station the other end.

LONDON TODAY

There is no doubt London has changed: a certain continental air pervades, people sit on pavements in inclement weather sipping coffee. Covent Garden piazza has thankfully been preserved - no vegetables but a lively shopping and eating area; Camden Lock is now a young people's preserve with a large market; Soho is no longer full of strip clubs - you are more likely to see men kissing and cuddling in public! The old financial area has been re-invented with a number of interesting and controversial buildings, and a few eyesores; Ludgate railway bridge no longer obscures the view of St. Paul's, though the city area is still as big a hodge-podge as it was in Wren's day! Young people who were born in the suburbs seem now to prefer to live in Central London again, I can understand that...that's life!

THE STREETS OF LONDON

London was no more than a swamp (*Llyn-dyn* in Celtic means a stronghold by the marsh) when the Romans first pitched camp on the northside of the Thames in AD 43, and built their town: it was called *Londinium* and was located between the Tower as it is now, and where the River Fleet used to enter the Thames close by the present Blackfriars Bridge. They built the first wooden bridge across the Thames (at the bisection of the town area) and a stone wall which, if it had been built a century earlier, might have stopped the warrior queen Boudicca from burning the town. Londinium was the heart of the Roman province of *Britannia* and the capital; it had a very large prestigious basilica (a Roman law court building) and forum (market place) which would encompass Gracechurch Street. Like so much of London, the street names tell the story: 'Walbrook' was once a small stream which ran through the centre of the Roman town.

When the legions finally withdrew in AD 410 after the collapse of the Roman Empire, civilization declined; the Walbrook flooded again and the town fell into ruins. For an idea of how London looked then visit the Museum of London (D2 32).

Overrun by Angles, Saxons and Jutes, the British fled westwards to Wales leaving what then became known as *Angleland* (England) to the invaders. Although the invaders were heathens it did not take long before Christianity had gained a footing and churches began to appear: St.Paul's was founded in the year 604 and a monastery was established at Westminster. London's importance only began to recover during the reign (871-901) of King Alfred the Great: he made London habitable again. Alfred built a navy which tussled with and beat the Danish and Norse pirates who were rampaging continuously up creeks and rivers. Eventually when peace came the Danes were allowed to settle and Canute became the King - he was also King of Denmark. The Strand (F5 31) - then a suburb of London - and Southwark on the other side of the Thames were inhabited by the Danes.

FRENCH CONNECTION

Having spent a great deal of his early life in Normandy, Edward the Confessor was enamoured with the Norman style of building, which was an extension of the Romanesque. He established the early palace and abbey at Westminster, where he was crowned. He died in 1066 and the Norsemen or Normans who had adopted the French language arrived and William the Conqueror became King. He built the Tower of London - the White Tower - (see page 49) which still stands today. Probably one of the finest examples of the Norman-style of church building to be seen in the city is the church of St.Bartholomew the Great (C2 32). The French contribution to architecture and in particular to the building of cathedrals with stone roofs gradually culminated in the pointed Gothic style, and with the establishment of English-Gothic architecture.

Today it is difficult to imagine that the Houses of Parliament stand on what was in those days the small island of Thorney, the site of the early Westminster Abbey which Henry III demolished in 1205, when centuries of construction commenced on the building of the Abbey (E4 39) as we see it now.

MEDIEVAL TIMES

London had become three districts during this period: the City, Westminster and Southwark - which was connected to the city by the old stone London Bridge which lasted from 1209-1756, and had houses

OLD LONDON BRIDGE BY CLAUDE DE JONGH

and even a chapel built on top of it. Southwark was renowned for brothels and other entertainments: bull and bear rings were attractions long before Shakespeare's 'Globe' arrived in 1599, and it has arrived again, thanks to the years of endeavour by the American actor Sam Wanamaker who finally managed to get the theatre reconstructed close to the original site (D6 32).

Westminster housed the royal residence until it finally became the home of Parliament during Henry VIII's reign. Westminster Hall is all that is left to see of this original building if you do visit the Houses of Parliament. In the City the merchants established their guilds and they elected the first mayor of London in 1188; the City has remained autonomous since that time. There were also large priories at Blackfriars and Whitefriars - friars unlike monks were in the beginning working Christians who tended the sick and needy; in *The Canterbury Tales* Chaucer gives another view. Henry VIII banned monks and friars and unfortunately he knocked down many beautiful abbeys and monasteries.

GROWTH - FIRE - PROSPERITY

Towards the end of the Tudor lineage London's population had reached almost 200,000. Henry VIII had laid out Hyde Park and St.James's Park and moved the royal palace to Whitehall, but it was his daughter Elizabeth I who was probably responsible for the growth of the city: she granted the East India Company the monopoly of trade with the eastern hemisphere. This was the beginning of London as a financial centre. After abolishing the monarchy and to a certain degree self-inflicting Oliver Cromwell on themselves, the British people returned to monarchy with restrictions. However, Cromwell had allowed Jews to settle in London after centuries of exclusion, and this was certainly good for finances and the country. Then after a terrible plague, fire broke out in 1666 destroying most of the city and the old St. Paul's. The phoenix was Christopher Wren (see page 12), whose plan for the city was never allowed to come to fruition as people hastened to rebuild without a great deal of attention to planning. The Monument (G5 33) was designed by Wren and was erected near where the fire started; who could ever dispute the uplift that St. Paul's gives to the spirits of Londoners?

When the 18th century dawned the Bank of England had been founded for just six years and London had become the largest financial centre in the world, overtaking Amsterdam. Residential districts grew in Lincoln's Inn and Covent Garden, which already had the marvellous Inigo Jones piazza and St.Paul's church. London's famous landmark squares were also laid out as the century proceeded. The trade with the east brought the phenomenon of coffee houses, where business was often transacted.

In 1811 the country had a Prince Regent (later George IV) and a certain architectural style which is attributed to the architect John Nash who was reponsible for one of London's joys - the lovely Cumberland Terrace (H3 21) that overlooks Regent's Park. The Haymarket Theatre (D6 30) and also a considerable part of Buckingham Palace (A3 38) are attributed to him.

DICKENS' LONDON

London during Queen Victoria's reign was the capital of a huge and much envied empire, and the scene of a great deal of squalor - not a cardboard city then and certainly not as jolly as a Christmas card, but without doubt the inspiration for the art and heart of Charles Dickens. Many of his locations are still very much the same as they were in his day, particularly around the Temple area (H4 31). The River Thames was spanned by most of the bridges we see today and with the advent of the steam engine, railways were constructed enabling London to spread even further afield. The villages of Islington, Hampstead and Highgate were no longer separate, yet strangely if you visit them, a certain amount of village atmosphere still prevails. The central station terminuses were built - St. Pancras (E3 23) is a monument itself to the steam age and is Londons finest station.

Another man who never forgot his roots in Lambeth (A5 40) was Charlie Chaplin whose autobiography vividly describes his life in south London at the end of the 19th century, when music halls and pubs became escapes from the tedium of work. Although many theatres have disappeared there are plenty of pubs to get the feel of life in those days.

MILLENNIUM

By the beginning of the 20th century London's population had reached 6.5 million, larger than Paris and New York. It had spread far and wide due to the underground system that enabled people to commute quickly to central London. Although the city was unscathed by the Great War, much of the city of London was destroyed later when the Second World War started. Hitler attempted to demoralize the British people with his 'blitzkreig' which set London's East End and docks alight: the red skies of those autumn nights of 1940 are indelible on my memory.

Reconstruction was slow after the war and many gaps still remained until recent times. The Festival of Britain in 1951 inaugurated new forms of building and architecture - the Festival Hall is an example of this period. Within the the labyrinth of the city you will discover many fine buildings both old and new. You cannot always see many of the features because the buildings are still so close to each other, and I guess this is the character of London. It obviously helped the IRA who managed to plant their bombs and create mayhem.

What happens next? People are returning to the centre to live. Perhaps the Bank of England will be abolished and turned into a fun palace. I'm joking - but you never know!

> *For a good view over London's roof-tops, walk up Primrose Hill (E1 21). A plaque at the top explains the panorama for you.*

THE BRITISH MUSEUM

Map reference E2 31 Set in Bloomsbury this is truly a great museum - in the top league with few rivals - and it is the most popular museum in London. This superb building houses an immense collection of treasures from all over the world. It was built in 1857 in the neo-classical style by the architect Robert Smirke, and if you approach the museum from the south, you view a magnificent Ionic-colonnaded façade with a pediment containing allegorical sculptures that represent the progress of the human race in Art and Science etc. The museum was founded in 1753, when physician Sir Hans Sloane's library and varied collection of over 80,000 objects, including plants, fossils, coins and manuscripts, was purchased by the government with proceeds of a public lottery. The first home of the museum from the was on the present site in a 17th century mansion known as Montague House, which disappeared when the existing building was constructed. The azure, round 'Reading Room' which is absolutely magnificent was finished in 1857 and is the work of Smirke's younger brother Sydney. In the centre of the area - originally an open quadrangle - Smirke built his dome which is over 140 feet in diameter, and is wider than the dome of St.Peters in Rome. With the removal of the 'British Library' to St.Pancras and the beginning of the new century, a glass roof was constructed to span the two acre courtyard and dome, it has been renamed the 'Great Court'.

THE MARVELS OF ATHENS

 There is no doubt that the *'Elgin Marbles'*, are one of the museums greatest attractions, and it is very easy to understand why the Greeks would like to see them returned to Athens. Collected by the Earl of Elgin in 1801, they were sold to the British government in 1816. Originally these sculptures, reckoned by many people to be the greatest classical carvings in the world, adorned the 438 BC Parthenon - the Temple of Athene Parthenos (the virgin) - which overlooks Athens from the Acropolis hill. It is quite likely they would have been broken up if Elgin had not acquired them - who knows? You can view these wonders on the ground floor in the Duveen Gallery, which was purpose built in 1938 to exhibit them.

MADNESS IN GREAT ONES

Staring eyes have always seemed to me to be linked with some form of madness: I think of Hitler, Mosley and other such gangsters. The bust of the Roman emperor Augustus (27BC - AD14) is striking for his piercing eyes inlaid with marble and glass, and his posture. He was not mad though: related to Julius Caeser, he became Rome's first Emperor and set about undoing military dictatorship and making the empire more constitutional. See room 70.

METALLIC BEAUTY

In the centre of room 33 is the 8th century figure of Tara a goddess from Sri Lanka in gilded bronze. The sculpting of material is sheer beauty.

THE MUMMIES OF EGYPT

Children always seem to have a strange fascination for the bandaged mummies inside their exotic cases, and there are rooms full of them to contemplate. I was frightened as a small child (pre-Hammer) when I was taken to the cinema, so I would not be the night watchman in this gallery. Here too, is *'Ginger'*, a man born over 5000 years ago, who was near as perfectly preserved in hot desert sand - he was given his name because of the colour of his hair.

SUTTON HOO TREASURE

In 1939 the remains of a 7th century ship were accidently found in a Suffolk field. The ship contained the treasures of an Anglo-Saxon king, who had been buried with his worldly acquisitions, including many interesting pieces of jewellery in gold and enamel which are well preserved and worth seeking out. His helmet is really stunning and although once fragmented it has been very carefully restored.

REFLECTION

With such a vast selection you have to make your own choice. Here are a few that might interest you: an amazing 1585 ship clock (the dial is at the foot of the main mast) made in Prague, elegant Chinese porcelain, the Roman *'Lycurgus Cup'* in green glass that changes ruby-red in light and with wine, Isle of Lewis 12th century chessmen, Venetian glass, amazing collections of coins, and the *'Rosetta Stone'*. Drawings by Dürer, Michelangelo, Watteau, Claude Lorrain, and Turner are not necessarily on display but they can be viewed.

The Museum shop is an ideal place to buy presents or souvenirs to remind you of your visit to London. Prints, scarves, books, jewellery, and replicas of many of the museums sculptures are on sale.

Once inside the museum obtain a museum floor plan; you will need it!

GROUND FLOOR
GREEK & ROMAN
Including Bassae sculpture, the Nereid Monument - Sculptures from the Parthenon.
WESTERN ASIA
Ancient Palestine - Assyrian sculpture - Khorsabad, Nimrud, and Nineveh palace reliefs.
EGYPTIAN SCULPTURE
ORIENTAL COLLECTIONS
China, South and Southeast Asia - Amaravati sculpture - Islamic art.
ETHNOGRAPHY
The Mexican Gallery
THE READING ROOM
BASEMENT
GREEK and ROMAN
Architecture - Greek Sculpture - Ephesus
WESTERN ASIA
Ishtar Temple - Assyrian art.
UPPER FLOORS
PREHISTORIC & ROMANO-BRITISH
Stone Age (mezzanine) - Prehistory - Roman Britain
MEDIEVAL, RENAISSANCE and MODERN
Medieval tiles and pottery - clocks & watches - Waddesdon Bequest -
Europe 15th, 18th, 19th centuries -
Europe & America 20th century.
WESTERN ASIA Ancient Iran, Anatolia - Syria - Nimrud ivories - South Arabia
EGYPT Mummies - Tomb paintings and Papyri - Egypt and Africa - Coptic Egypt.
COINS and MEDALS
GREEK and ROMAN
Rome: City & Empire -
Pre-Roman Empire Italy -
Ancient Cyprus -
Greeks in Southern Italy.
PRINTS & DRAWINGS
ORIENTAL COLLECTIONS
Japanese Galleries.

Monday-Wednesday, Saturday, Sunday 10.00-17.30,
Thursday and Friday 10.00-20.30 *Free*
The Great Court is open late most evenings except Sunday for access to the restaurants etc.

APSLEY HOUSE, WELLINGTON MUSEUM G2 37
149 Piccadilly, W1. Built in 1778 by the Adam brothers in red brick, and refaced later in stone with the addition of a corinthian portico when the Iron Duke bought the house from his brother after his famous victory at Waterloo. Until his death in 1852, a banquet was held in the house to commemorate his finest hour. Filled with pictures, porcelain, silver, plate and other relics of the Duke. Probably the most singularly interesting item is the larger than life nude statue of his adversary Napoleon: one room of the house is decorated like a military tent of that era.
Tuesday - Sunday 11.00 - 17.00.   *Charge*

BANK OF ENGLAND MUSEUM F3 33
Bartholomew Lane, EC2. Chronicling monetary
 history this museum resides within the walls of the great city bank. Models, bank notes, gold bars and the complexities of exchanging money and dealing on the foreign exchanges will interest young budding traders.
Monday - Friday 10.00 - 17.00.   *Free*

CLOCKMAKER'S MUSEUM E3 33
Guildhall, Aldermanbury, EC2. Attached to the Guildhall is this small museum. Watches, clocks and the chronometers used at sea to establish the position of longitude are here: includes John Harrison's H5.
Monday - Friday 9.30 - 17.00.   *Free*

COURTAULD INSTITUTE GALLERIES E3 41
Strand, WC2. Situated in Somerset House, this is a superb collection of Impressionist and Post-Impressionist paintings and many other works bequeathed to the University of London. The finest of its kind in Britain, the collection includes works by Renoir, Degas, Manet, Monet, Seurat, Gauguin and Van Gogh, as well as Rubens and Van Dyck.
Mondays - Saturdays 10.00 - 18.00.
Sunday 14.00 - 18.00.   *Charge*

DALÍ UNIVERSE G2 39
South Bank. Over 500 extraordinary works created by the Spanish surrealist artist Salvador Dalí, including his *Mae West Lips Sofa, Buste de Femme Retrospectif,* and *Nobility of Time* sculptures. Also on view is the oil painting produced for the Alfred Hitchcock film *Spellbound..........* mesmerizing!   *Daily 10.00 - 17.30 Charge*

DICKENS HOUSE MUSEUM G6 23
48 Doughty Street, WC1. From 1837-39, Dickens lived in this four-floored terraced house and wrote his novels *Oliver Twist* and *Nicholas Nickleby* during that period. His manuscripts, photographs, and lantern slides etc. are on view.
Monday - Saturday 10.00 - 17.00.   *Charge*

DESIGN MUSEUM D6 48
Shad Thames, SE1 2YD. A rather austere building dedicated to 20-21st century design and focusing on everyday mass produced objects from motorbikes to household gadgets. *Daily 11.30 - 18.00. Charge*

GUARDS MUSEUM C3 38
Wellington Barracks, Birdcage Walk, SW1. The Guards regiments were founded in the 17th century and their history is recalled with their weapons, uniforms, trophies and personal belongings.
Daily 10.00 - 16.00.   *Charge*

HANDEL HOUSE MUSEUM H4 29
25 Brook Street, W1 Music and interior decorations recreate the time from 1723-59 when the Royal Fireworks composer Georg Friedrich Händel lived, worked and died in this house. *Tues, Weds, Fris, Sats, 10.00-18.00, Thurs 20.00 Suns 12.00-18.00 Charge*

HAYWARD GALLERY G1 39
South Bank, SE1. Adjoining the Queen Elizabeth Hall, the gallery is used for major art exhibitions. Always interesting displays, which is more than you can say for the exterior of the building.
Daily 10.00 - 18.00, Tues & Weds 20.00 Charge

IMPERIAL WAR MUSEUM A5 40
Lambeth Road, SE1. Once part of a lunatic asylum called 'Bedlam', the museum illustrates the history of the two world wars and also more recent combat operations involving Britain. You can experience what it was like in the trenches and in London's East End during the Blitz. Large collections of weapons and equipment, decorations, uniforms (Brezhnev's and General Schwarkopf's), photographs, paintings, and full size aircraft suspended from the ceiling.
Daily 10.00 - 18.00   *Free*

JEWISH MUSEUM H1 21
129-131 Albert Street, N1. Situated in Camden in a stylish extended townhouse you will find a collection of Jewish antiquities that illustrate both the private and the public religious life and history of the Jewish community in Britain. *Mons-Thurs 10.00-16.00. Closed Bank & Jewish Holidays. Charge*

LEIGHTON HOUSE C4 34
12 Holland Park Road, Kensington W14. Home of the celebrated Victorian artist Lord Leighton, who lived here until his death in 1896. Permanently on display are examples of High Victorian art with works by Leighton, Burne-Jones and Millais. The house is renowned for the beautiful Arab Hall, an authentic reconstruction of a Moorish palace banqueting hall. Fine period rooms of Victorian furniture, a collection of William de Morgan pottery and an attractive garden. Evening concerts.
Monday - Saturday 11.00 - 17.00.   *Free*

LONDON CANAL MUSEUM F2 23
12-13 New Wharf Road, N1 9RT. The story of the canals and the people who lived on the narrow boats.
Tuesday - Sunday 10.00 - 16.30.   *Charge*

LONDON TRANSPORT MUSEUM F4 31
Covent Garden WC2. In the flower market building of Covent Garden. This interesting museum illustrates the development of London's transport system with historic buses, trams, trolleybuses, and rail vehicles. *Daily 10.00 - 18.00*   *Charge*

MUSEUM OF LONDON D2 32
Barbican, London Wall, EC2. An intriguing display that defines the history, topography and rich heritage of London from prehistoric times to the present day. Roman remains, models of the Roman forum and baths, Anglo-Saxon material, furniture and clothing from Tudor and Stuart times, reconstructed shops and offices of Victorian and Edwardian days are just a few of the imaginative displays to be seen. Always attracting attention is the magnificent Lord Mayor's golden state coach and the Art-Deco elevator which used to whisk you to the restaurant at Selfridges.
Tuesday - Saturday 10.00 - 17.50,   *Free*
Sundays 12.00 - 17.50.   *Open Bank Holidays*

NATIONAL ARMY MUSEUM E3 45
Royal Hospital Rd, Chelsea, SW3. Imaginatively recording the story of British, Indian, and colonial land forces from Tudor times to the present day. Uniforms, weapons and personal relics of some great military leaders. Over 62,000 French, Prussian and English soldiers were killed at Waterloo in 1815. You can see a model of the battle and a film of it.
Daily 10.00 - 17.30   *Free*

NATIONAL GALLERY   D6 30

Trafalgar Square, WC2. Situated in the domain of London's pigeons, the gallery holds an unequalled collection representing the European schools of painting and it is particularly rich in examples of Dutch and Italian works. There is also a large selection of British paintings from the works of Hogarth to Turner. Modern paintings are not on display here, for the cut-off year is 1900. Colourful works like Van Gogh's *Sunflowers*, the last Turner paintings and his *Fighting Temeraire*, Renoir's *Umbrellas*, and Seurat's *Bathers at Asnières* are all here. There are also some marvellous dreamy Claude Lorrain canvases, the classic *Haywain* by Constable and the *Rokeby Venus* by Velázquez.
Monday - Saturday 10.00 - 18.00, Wednesday 20.00,
Sunday 12.00 - 18.00   *Free*

NATIONAL PORTRAIT GALLERY   D6 38

St. Martin's Place, WC2.
Interesting and often topical, this gallery tucked into the side of the National Gallery always holds your attention. Shakespeare to the Rolling Stones, that is the variety you get. Here are a few: all the Kings and Queens, John Donne, Cromwell, Nell Gwyn, the Brönte sisters, Lily Langtry, Byron, and Bernard Shaw. A couple of my

favourites are Noel Coward, and the great Manchester United footballer Bobby Charlton.
Mons-Sats 10.00-18.00, Suns 12.00-18.00. Free

NATURAL HISTORY MUSEUM   A5 36

Cromwell Rd. South Kensington, SW7. Built in

1880 in the romanesque style, this fine, colourful terracotta building has zoological decorations along its wide facade. The departments incorporate Botany, Entomology, Minerology, Paleontology, Zoology and the Museum of Geology, renamed the 'Earth Galleries', and has some interesting features - an escalator ride through a portion of a rotating globe to the 'Power Within' exhibition which explains volcanos and earthquakes. The film *Jurassic Park* stimulated interest in dinosaurs, and this museum has the real bones and some absorbing tableaux the children will enjoy.
Mons-Sats 10.00 - 17.50, Suns 10.00 - 17.50. Free

QUEEN'S GALLERY. THE   A4 38

Buckingham Palace Rd. SW1. Formerly the private chapel of Buckingham Palace, now used as an exhibition gallery, changing annually to display to the public a small part of the vast royal collection which includes famous artists' works, drawings, photographs and other works of art.   *Charge*
Opening Hours 09.30 - 17.30   Last Entrance 16.30
Entrance by Timed Tickets   ☎ *020 7766 7301*

ROYAL ACADEMY OF ARTS   B6 30

Burlington House, Piccadilly, W1. Founded in 1768 by Joshua Reynolds whose statue stands in the courtyard, the Academy is famous for its annual Summer Exhibition from May to September, which exhibits the works of living artists. Other exhibitions are also held throughout the year.
Daily 10.00 - 18.00   *Charge*

SCIENCE MUSEUM   B4 36

Exhibition Rd. SW7. I always enjoyed my trips as a child to this museum; it was one of the first to allow you to interact in the discovery process. I have no doubt that children today find this museum one of the most interesting to visit. The museum traces many of the great achievements in the history and development of science and industry, and displays on five floors some of the original machines and equipment: steam engines like Stephenson's *Rocket* along with modern prototype locomotives. Mitchell's famous *Schneider Trophy Seaplane*, the forerunner of the Spitfire; the *Apollo 10* command module; veteran cars, and many other experiences that you can participate in: you can fly a plane, be an air traffic controller, mix and record music etc.
IMAX cinema book on ☎ *0870 870 4771*   *Charge*
Museum opens daily 10.00 - 18.00,   *Free*

SOANE MUSEUM   G3 31

13 Lincoln's Inn Fields, WC2. Son of a bricklayer Sir John Soane (1753-1837) an architect who was responsible for the windowless (for security) exterior wall of the Bank of England. His art collection and atmospheric house is filled like a magician's box with unforeseen revelations: Hogarth, Canaletto, Watteau, Reynolds, Turner and others are here along with Egyptian and Roman antiquities.
First Tuesday of the month 18.00 - 21.00,
Tuesday - Saturday 10.00 - 17.00.   *Free*

TATE BRITAIN   E1 47

Millbank, SW1. Facing the Thames, this gallery contains British art from Tudor times onwards; the Turner collection is magnificent and includes his cerulean Venice paintings. You can view Hogarth, Constable, William Blake, the Pre-Raphaelites, Walter Sickert, etc., and sculptures by Henry Moore and Jacob Epstein. The restaurant is also notable, but it is unfortunately not open in the evenings.
Open Daily 10.00 - 17.50   *Free*

TATE MODERN   C6 32

Bankside, SE1. Opened in 2000, the original Turbine Hall of the renovated Bankside power station makes an impressive introduction to this eclectic collection of international arts of the 20-21st centuries, includes works by Francis Bacon, Cézanne, Bonnard, Dali, Roy Lichtenstein, Magritte, Matisse, Mirò, Picasso etc., and sculptures by Rodin and Constantin Brancusi. On the top floor is a café which has fine views across London.   *Suns - Thurs 10.00 - 18.00,*
Fris - Sats 10.00 - 22.00.   *Free*

VICTORIA AND ALBERT MUSEUM   B5 36

Cromwell Rd, South Kensington, SW7. One of the world's great and inspirational art collections with displays of fine and applied art of all countries, periods and styles. There are the great cartoons (tapestry patterns) executed by Raphael in 1516 for Pope Leo X, a large number of works by Constable, Tiffany glass, Limoges enamels, Post-Classical sculpture, Indian art, a Frank Lloyd Wright gallery, and at the rear of the museum the Morris and Gamble rooms, which are also worth seeking out. They used to be restaurant rooms.   *Mons 12.00 - 15.45,*
Tues - Suns 10.00 - 17.45, Weds 18.30 - 21.30. Free

WALLACE COLLECTION   F3 29

Manchester Sq. W1. A superb collection of works of art from all periods and from many lands especially France: pictures - Watteau's *La Toilette* - and 17th-18th century porcelain and furniture. There are also many examples of European and Oriental arms and armour, terracotta, jewellery, bronzes, and pictures by Flemish, Spanish and Italian masters. *The Laughing Cavalier* by Hals - the man that made lace come alive on canvas - is here!
Monday - Saturday 10.00 - 17.00,
Sunday 14.00 - 17.00.   *Free*

PLACES OF INTEREST

ALBERT MEMORIAL A3 36
Kensington Gore, SW7. This memorial was not of Albert's wish; nevertheless it is very impressive and it is, if anything, a memorial to Victorian arts and crafts. The Prince Consort (1819-61) sits under a canopy holding the catalogue to the Great Exhibition of 1851, beneath him is a high relief frieze of 200 figures: musicians, poets, painters etc.

BANQUETING HOUSE E3 39
Whitehall, SW1. This was the only part of Whitehall Palace to survive the Great Fire. Designed in the Palladian style by Inigo Jones, it dates from 1622 and is noted for the fine allegorical ceiling paintings.

BRITISH LIBRARY, THE D4 22
96 Euston Rd. NW1. Not an attractive exterior but the brickwork does blend with the superb station adjacent. In the forecourt is an imposing bronze statue representing Sir Isaac Newton reducing the universe to mathematical dimensions, by Sir Eduardo Paolozzi. The library holds millions of books and manuscripts. It is a library of deposit and receives a copy of every publication printed in Britain. Many works of art are on display throughout the library including in the entrance hall a marble statue of *Shakespeare* by Roubiliac dated 1758. There are three exhibition galleries where you will find treasures like the 7th century *Lindisfarne Gospels* (beautiful Celtic illuminated manuscripts), the *Magna Carta*, the *Gutenberg Bible* (the first printed book), and a 16th century Mercator Atlas.
Daily Monday-Saturday 9.30-18.00, Tuesday 20.00, Saturday 17.00. Sundays 11.00 - 17.00 *Free*

BBC EXPERIENCE A2 30
Portland Place, W1. Inside Broadcasting House, the BBC's home since 1932. The semi-guided tour shows how your favourite programmes are produced. Take part in a radio drama, read the weather, see the first TV pictures from Alexander Palace and hear great wartime speeches. *Information* ☎ *0870 6030304.*
Daily 10.00 - 16.30, Mondays 13.30 - 16.30. Charge

BRITISH AIRWAYS LONDON EYE G2 39
South Bank. This ferris wheel turns half-hourly. Climbing to 450 feet, the 33 capsules encompass wonderful atmospheric views over the river and London. Box Office County Hall ☎ *0870 5000 600*
Daily 09.00-17.30. May-Sept 09.00-21.30 Charge

BUCKINGHAM PALACE A3 38
The Mall, SW1. The London residence of the Queen the forecourt of which is guarded by the colourful sentries of the Guards Division, and the scene of the daily ceremony of The Changing of the Guard.
Daily May - August 11.30, weather permitting. Alternate days September - April.
On August 7th 1993, the Queen for the first time opened the Palace State Apartments to the public. Designed by John Nash for George IV in 1826, the apartments contain beautiful brocades, furniture, clocks and paintings. The ticket office is in the Mall near the Victoria Memorial, on the Green Park side by Constitution Hill. Advance booking advisable.
Open from 7th August 9.30 - 17.30 approximately until the end of September. *Charge*

CABINET WAR ROOMS D3 38
Clive Steps, King Charles St. SW1.
The famous Map Room and the 21-roomed bunker and nerve centre used by Winston Churchill and his cabinet during World War Two: preserved with sound effects. *Daily April - August 9.30 - 18.00, September - March inclusive 10.00 - 18.00. Charge*

CHESHIRE CHEESE, YE OLDE B3 32
Wine Office Court, Fleet St. EC4. An ancient hostelry, rebuilt 1667, said to have been frequented by Dr. Johnson, Goldsmith and many other literary celebrities. Sawdust, uneven floors and a mention in Dicken's *Tale of Two Cities.*

CHURCHES OF INTEREST
ALL HALLOWS BY THE TOWER B4 48
Byward Street, EC3. A church was founded here in AD 675, but the present restored building dates from the 13th and 15th centuries. The church registers record the baptism of William Penn and the marriage of John Quincy Adams, later the sixth president of the United States. There are some good brasses in this church.

BROMPTON ORATORY C4 36
Brompton Road, SW7. The London oratory of St. Philip Neri. A Roman Catholic church with a wide nave built in the Baroque style in 1884, and noted for its music and choral recitals.

ST. BARTHOLOMEW THE GREAT C2 32
West Smithfield, EC1. An interesting and historic Norman building, once an Augustinian priory, and the second oldest church in London. Unfortunately the nave was a victim of the Dissolution and today it is nowhere near its original length. At one period, the Lady Chapel was used as a print shop where Benjamin Franklin came to work. The painter Hogarth, who lived nearby, was baptised here.

ST. HELEN'S, BISHOPSGATE H3 33
Great St.Helen's,, EC3. A survivor of an IRA bomb attack in 1993, the blitz and the Fire of London, this is one of the most pleasurable of the city churches. The 13th century nun's church has parallel naves, indicating that there were two churches - one was a benedictine nunnery. The church contains many monuments to city worthies, and is well known for its music.

ST. MARTIN-IN-THE-FIELDS E6 31
Trafalgar Square, WC2. Dating from 1726 this influential work by James Gibb has a temple portico and a 185 foot steeple; inside there is some very fine Italian plasterwork on the ceiling. Renowned for excellent free lunchtime concerts, winter candlelit concerts, brass rubbing and for the Café in the Crypt.

ST. PAUL'S, COVENT GARDEN E5 31
Covent Garden, WC2. Many parts of the Covent Garden area were owned by the Earl of Bedford: he commisioned Inigo Jones to build the Piazza and the church which dates from 1638, although it has been altered slightly when it was restored. Known as the 'Actors Church', there are many memorials to entertainment personalities: Charles Cochrane, Ivor Novello, Vivien Leigh, Noel Coward, Boris Karloff.

SOUTHWARK CATHEDRAL F6 33
Montague Close, SE1. A fine Gothic building that is second only to Westminster Abbey; the choir and chapel were built in 1207. Near the Shakespeare memorial is a stained-glass window depicting scenes from his plays. John Harvard, the founder of the American University, was baptised here in 1607: so a chapel is dedicated to him. The new Chapter House contains a Pizza Express restaurant.

CLEOPATRA'S NEEDLE F6 31
Victoria Embankment, WC2. A pink granite obelisk 68 feet high, presented by the Egyptian viceroy in 1819, and floated here by sea in 1878. With a companion monolith in Central Park, New York, it stood at Heliopolis in 1500 BC.

DR.JOHNSON'S HOUSE A3 22
17 Gough Square, EC4. The great man lived here from 1748 to 1759 where he wrote many of his works including his great Dictionary.
Monday - Saturday 11.00 - 17.30 *Charge*

ELEANOR CROSS E6 31
Charing X Station, WC2. Many Gothic crosses were erected by Edward 1st where Queen Eleanor's coffin was set down on its route to Westminster. This Victorian replica stands east of the original location.

FLEET STREET A4 32
EC4. Named after the old Fleet River, now a sewer running from Hampstead to Blackfriars into the Thames. It was "The Street of Ink." The newspapers have all gone now, but the street still has character.

GEORGE INN F1 41
77 Borough High St. SE1. The surviving example of an old galleried inn well worth a visit. Famous as a coaching terminus in the 18th-19th centuries, it has a good restaurant with atmosphere.

GLOBE CENTRE D6 32
New Globe Walk, Bankside, SE1. We have to thank

American actor, Sam Wanamaker, for the persistence of his vision to rebuild the Globe near to the original site of the theatre where Shakespeare produced his plays. There is an exhibition, and during the summer the open-air theatre will demonstrate theatre as it was in Shakespeare's time. The restaurants have good river views and occasional music. *Daily May-September 9.00-12.15, 14.00-16.00, October-April 10.00-17.00. Charge*

GRAY'S INN H1 31
Gray's Inn Rd. WC2. London has four great Inns of Court with the right to admit lawyers to practise as barristers in the English courts. They are Middle Temple, Inner Temple, Lincoln's Inn and Gray's Inn.
Monday - Friday 10.00-16.00. Gardens 12.00-14.00.

GUILDHALL E3 33
King Street, Cheapside, EC2. For more than 800 years the centre of civic government; the first mayor was elected in 1192. Begun in about 1411, only part of the walls, the Great Hall and crypt survive from that time. The Great Hall with monuments of famous people is used for the election of Lord Mayor and Sheriffs and other gatherings. The eastern half of the 15th century crypt is notable for its six clustered pillars of blue Purbeck marble. A new building adjoining now houses:
The Guildhall Art Gallery which displays works from the 16c to the present day: unearthed during building are the remains of a Roman amphitheatre.
Mon- Sats 10.00-17.00, Suns 12.00-16.00 Charge
The Library has a unique collection of prints and books on the history of the city.
Open from 9.00 - 17.00 Monday - Saturday.

HMS BELFAST B5 48
Symons Wharf, Vine Lane, SE1. A famous World War Two cruiser permanently moored near Tower Bridge. Part of the Imperial War Museum the 11,500-ton cruiser played a leading role in European waters.
March-Oct. 10-18.00, Nov-Feb closes 16.00. Charge

HORSE GUARDS E1 39
Whitehall, SW1. The Horse Guards building with its handsome clocktower was built in 1753. Here you see mounted sentries of the Household Cavalry: the Life Guards (scarlet tunics) and the Blues and Royals (blue tunics). The spectacle of the 'Changing of the Guard', takes place at 11.00 weekdays and 10.00 on Sundays. Approached through the archway is the extensive open drill ground Horse Guards Parade, which is the scene of the annual Trooping of the Colour ceremony before the Queen in early June.

HOUSES OF PARLIAMENT E3 39
Palace of Westminster, SW1. Seat of the supreme legislature of the United Kingdom, a late-Gothic style building designed by Sir Charles Barry on the site of the former royal palace. The House of Lords, a lavishly decorated Gothic chamber, contains the throne of the Sovereign, the Woolsack, the seat of the Lord Chancellor and red leather benches for the peers. The House of Commons, rebuilt after war damage in its original style, has the Speakers chair and parallel rows of green leather benches for members. In the large Victoria Tower - 336 feet to the top of the pinnacles - are stored many Parliamentary records. A part of the old 14th century Palace of Westminster to survive is Westminster Hall, which is renowned for its hammer-beam roof - it has been the scene of great historic events and trials.
Big Ben the Clock Tower, rising to 320 feet has four dials and houses the famous fourteen-ton bell which is struck hourly. When parliament is sitting there is a light above the clock. *To see Prime Ministers Question Time book well in advance.*
Monday - Thursday 9.00 - 18.00, Friday 16.30, when Parliament is in session. In recesses 10.00 - 17.00. For the Visitors Gallery (PM's Q.T.) ☎ *7219 4272*

JEWEL TOWER E4 39
Old Palace Yard, SW1. Another survival from the old Palace of Westminster built originally to house the King's private wealth and so used until the death of Henry VIII. Now a museum showing relics of the old palace and an exhibition of Parliament's history with a video. *Daily April - September 10.00 - 18.00, October - March 10.00 - 16.00 Tues - Suns. Charge*

KENSINGTON PALACE F2 35
Kensington Palace Gdns. W8. A Jacobean building, the former residence of the Sovereign from 1689 to 1760 and later altered as the home of George 1. Many of the apartments are used for relatives of the royal family. The State Apartments include rooms by Wren and Kent, with portraits, furniture, the royal dress collection and mementoes of Queen Victoria and Queen Mary, both of whom were born in the palace. This was Princess Diana's last London residence - when they first married, Prince Charles lived here with her. *Daily 10.00 - 18.00 Charge*
Mid October - mid March Weds - Suns 10.00 - 16.00

LAMBETH PALACE G5 39
Lambeth Road, SE1. The official residence of the Archbishop of Canterbury for over 700 years. The famous Great Hall and other rooms contain many manuscripts and incunabula (early printed books).
Only the gardens are open to the public, four times a year on Saturday afternoons.

LONDON AQUARIUM G3 39
County Hall, SE1. A spectacular display of aquatic life, with fishes and invertebrates from all over the world, including sharks, sea scorpions, sting rays and deadly piranhas. *Daily 10.00 - 18.00. Charge*

LONDON BRASS RUBBING CENTRE E6 31

St.Martins-in-the-Fields, Trafalger Square Replicas of many fine church brasses are available here for visitors to make their own brass rubbing, with instructions and the materials supplied if required.
Monday - Saturdays 10.00 - 18.00, Sundays 12.00 - 18.00. *Charge*

LONDON PLANETARIUM F1 29
Marylebone Rd. NW1. Adjoining Madam Tussauds in a dome shaped building where you can sit and see a spectacular reproduction of the night sky, as seen from any point on the earth's surface, projected on the hemispherical ceiling. Shows last 30 minutes.
Daily Monday - Friday 11.30 - 17.00, Saturday - Sunday 9.30 - 17.00 *Charge*

MADAME TUSSAUDS F1 29
Marylebone Rd., NW1. Renowned waxworks exhibition with figures of the famous and infamous from the past and present. The garden party, chamber of horrors and other striking tableaux.
Daily 9.00 - 17.30 *Charge*

Rock Circus C5 30
Piccadilly Circus, W1. This is also part of Tussauds and if rock and pop are part of your scene you might find this of interest - waxworks and music!
Daily 11.00 - 21.00. *Charge*

MANSION HOUSE F4 33
The Lord Mayor's official residence, renowned for the magnificent Egyptian Hall used for banquets. Underneath are prison cells where Emily Pankhurst, the suffragette, was once interned.

MARBLE ARCH E4 29
A triumphal arch at the NE corner of Hyde Park. Designed by John Nash, it was originally sited in front of Buckingham Palace, but was removed to the present position when the palace was extended. The medieval Tyburn Gallows once stood nearby.

NELSON'S COLUMN E6 31
Trafalgar Square.   Monument to Lord Nelson's victory at Trafalgar in 1805. A 167 foot high fluted Corinthian column made of granite by William Railton, topped by a 17 foot statue of the famous admiral. The bronze lions at the base were modelled by Sir Edwin Landseer.

OLD CURIOSITY SHOP G3 31
Portsmouth Street, WC2. In a turning off Kingsway, an antique and souvenir shop with a 16th century front, that claims to be the original *Old Curiosity Shop* made famous by Charles Dickens.

ROYAL COURTS OF JUSTICE H4 31
Strand, WC2. The Law Courts in a huge Gothic building with over 30 courts and public galleries. The Central Hall is notable for its fine rose window.

ROYAL EXCHANGE F4 33
Cornhill, EC3. Sir Thomas Gresham founded the Exchange in 1566. His crest, a grasshopper, is seen as the weathervane on the 180 foot high campanile. The courtyard and the ambulatory are often used for exhibitions. A carillon plays tunes at three hourly intervals from 9.00 - 18.00. *Free*
Monday - Friday 10.00 - 16.00, Sats 10.00 - 12.00

ROYAL HOSPITAL, CHELSEA F3 45
Royal Hospital Rd., SW3.   Founded in 1682 by Charles II for veteran and invalid soldiers. Originally designed by Wren with later building by Robert Adam and Sir John Soane. The "Chelsea Pensioners", of whom there are more than 500, wear traditional uniforms of scarlet frock coat in summer and dark blue in winter. The gardens are the scene of the annual Chelsea Flower Show.
Monday - Saturday 10.00 - 12.00, and 14.00 - 16.00. Sunday 14.00 - 16.00 *Free*

ROYAL MEWS A4 38
Buckingham Palace Road, SW1. Entered by an impressive Classical archway, the mews were built by John Nash, and house the Queen's unique collection of automobiles, coaches and carriages, as well as the coach horses. The main attraction is the fabulous Gold State coach which has been used for every Coronation since 1820.
Open from the end of March to the end of October except during state visits from 10.00 - 17.00
Ticket Sales ☎ 020 7766 7302 *Charge*

SHERLOCK HOLMES MUSEUM E6 21
221b Baker Street, NW1. A small popular museum that makes the most out of Sir Arthur Conan Doyle's fictional character. On the ground floor is Hudson's Restaurant for tea! *Daily 9.30 - 18.00* *Charge*

SPEAKERS CORNER E5 29
On the NE of Hyde Park near Marble Arch. Anyone can indulge in free speech without hindrance - other than hecklers - before a usually amused audience.

TEMPLE, THE A4 32
Fleet Street, EC4. Of the four Inns of Court of the legal profession in London, two are here, Middle Temple and Inner Temple, in a quiet traffic-free oasis of lovely gardens and Georgian buildings. Here too is the Round Church, built by the Knight Templars in the 12th century on the model of the church of the Holy Sepulchre in Jerusalem, with a rectangular Early English chancel added a century later. Above the east gate is Prince Henry's Room built in 1610.

TEMPLE OF MITHRAS E4 33
Queen Victoria St. EC4. Rebuilt remains of a Roman temple. The temple was used for the worship of the sun-god Mithras from about AD 90 to 350.

TOWER BRIDGE C6 48
A unique drawbridge across the Thames - a symbol of London. The bridge's twin bascules, each weighing about 1000 tons, are between two huge Gothic towers, connected near the top by a fixed glazed walkway with panoramic views, and standing 140 feet above high water level. The central span measures 200 feet and the suspension chains on either side 270 feet. The bascules carrying the roadway are raised hydraulically to permit the passage of large vessels.
Museum daily April - October 10.00 - 18.30.
November - March 9.30 - 18.00 *Charge*

WELLINGTON ARCH G2 37
Hyde Park Corner, W1. Triumphal arch built in 1825 by Decimus Burton topped by Adrian Jones's striking bronze quadriga, or four-horse chariot, which depicts *Peace Checking the Chariot of War.*
April - Sept 10.00 -18.00, (Oct 17.00, Nov 16.00), Wednesday - Sundays & Bank Hols. *Charge*

WESLEY'S HOUSE & CHAPEL F6 25
49 City Rd. EC1.   This is an 18th century chapel and Georgian town house where the founder of Methodism lived. Mrs Thatcher got married here!
Mons - Sats 10.00 - 16.00, Sunday 11.00.

WESTMINSTER ABBEY E4 39
Parliament Square, SW1.
Subject to the Sovereign, not the church through a dean and chapter, the Abbey has been the crowning place of all the English monarchs since William the Conqueror: here too most of them since Henry III are buried. There are tombs and monuments to statesmen, warriors, poets and men of letters. Of interest is the Coronation Chair, made for Edward I, and the Stone of  Scone beneath, and upon which the Kings of Scotland and every English monarch since Edward I have been crowned. Poet's Corner in the South Transept is where to find the *Grave of the Unknown Warrior*. Once meeting place of the House of Commons, the Chapter House dates from 1250. The architect of the twin towers was Nicholas Hawksmoor, a pupil of Wren. They date from 1745.
Daily 8.00 - 18.00, Wednesday 20.00. *Charge*

WESTMINSTER CATHEDRAL B5 38
Ashley Place, SW1. The central Roman Catholic church in England. Seat of the Cardinal Archbishop of Westminster. A large church built in 1903 in the Early Byzantine and the Romanesque styles with a pleasant piazza frontage. Built in alternate layers of red brick and portland stone it has a pleasing and unusual effect. The campanile, or tower is 273 feet high. *Daily 7.00 - 20.00. Charge to ascend the tower.*

CHRISTOPHER WREN'S LONDON

Christopher Wren was born in East Knoyle, Wiltshire in 1632. He went to Westminster School and then Oxford at the age of fourteen, where he studied mathematics and where later, at the age of 28, he became the Professor of Astronomy. In 1665, he spent six months in Paris studying architecture, the following year his opportunity came after the Fire of London had destroyed the city. He was asked to be the Surveyor-General and to prepare a master plan for the reconstruction of London. Unfortunately people began building very quickly and his plan for the whole city was not used: even today, the city is a haphazard muddle of buildings and alleys. We can only guess at the elegance and space his plan would have brought by marvelling at his great achievements: St. Paul's and Greenwich Hospital in London, and the Sheldonian theatre in Oxford. These reach heights of dignity and classicism which have set the standards in English Architecture. Wren lived until 1723; he was 91 when he died, proof that work kills nobody.

MONUMENT, THE   A4 48
Fish Street Hill, EC3.   Wren built this 62 metre (202 feet) high fluted Doric column in portland stone between 1671-7, to commemorate the Great Fire of 1666, which broke out in Pudding Lane nearby. Some 311 steps lead up to a caged balcony - underneath a spiky ball - from which there are some great views of the city.
Summer Monday - Friday 9.00 - 18.00,
Saturdays & Sundays 14.00 - 18.00, October - March
Monday - Saturday 9.00 - 16.00   *Charge*

ST. PAUL'S CATHEDRAL   D4 32
St. Paul's Churchyard, EC4.   Wren's majestic masterpiece, the largest and the most famous church in London. The beautiful dome reaches to a height of 110 metres (365 feet), and within the dome is the whispering gallery which has quite remarkable acoustic properties - try it out! Wren was 43 when the foundation stone was laid, and 79 when it was finished. The money to build the cathedral was raised by an importation tax on coal and wine coming in through London's docks.
Wren's sojourn in Paris quite clearly helped him to formulate his inspiration and enthusiasm for classical and renaissance architecture. His first model of the cathedral - which when rejected they say brought him to tears - can be viewed in the crypt, where there are also numerous tombs of famous men including Wren and Nelson, Wellington, and Lawrence of Arabia. The dome ceiling was painted by James Thornhill who was nearly killed executing his work, which depicts the life of St. Paul.
Many people will want to see *The Light of the World* by Holman Hunt, the Pre-Raphaelite painter; this you will find in the nave. In the south choir aisle is the only monument from the medieval St. Paul's that survived the fire, the tomb of the Poet-Dean John Donne, "No man is an Island…"whose love poems live on to this day.
Only the young in heart and body should attempt the experience of climbing to the top; you can go just underneath the ball and cross, there are 628 steps for you to mount - count them!
Monday - Saturday 8.30 - 16.00.   *Charge*

There is no doubt at all that Christopher Wren was a great architect. However much doubt has been cast by hand-writing experts over the past few years as to whether he was responsible for so many of London's city churches. The fact that a Wren church equals a tourist attraction is probably responsible for the myths. As the surveyor-general, he must have been the overall supervisor, but as for the nitty-gritties, he would surely have delegated to those working in his office to get so much work done in such a short time. Here is a list of churches in chronological order:
ST. MICHAEL, Cornhill.   1670-2.   **G4 33**
The nave is attributed to Wren.
ST. VEDAST, Foster Lane. 1670-3.   **D3 32**
ST. MARY AT HILL, St. Mary at Hill. 1670-6 **G5 33**
ST. MARY-LE-BOW, Cheapside.1670-83   **E4 33**
Damaged by the luftwaffe, Bow Church - the original cockney church - was restored after the war; the original *Bow Bells* as the story goes, recalled Dick Whittington as Lord Mayor.
ST. LAWRENCE, Gresham St. 1671-7   **E3 33**
ST. BRIDE'S, Fleet Street. 1671-1703.   **E4 33**
When it was blitzed in 1941, Roman and Saxon remains were discovered; these can be viewed in the crypt. The telescopic steeple (68 metres or 226 feet) is Wren's tallest parish church steeple.It is said that it has been the blueprint for many wedding cakes!
ST. MAGNUS, Lower Thames St.,1671-1705. **G5 33**
ST. STEPHEN WALBROOK, 1672-1717.   **F4 33**
Many people regard this church as his finest - a mini St. Paul's. The Samaritans - who help people through their problems by listening - were founded here in 1953 by the rector Chad Varah: the poignant memorial to him is a telephone in a glass box. Another recent addition is the central white stone altar by Henry Moore.
ST. JAMES, Garlick Hill. 1674-87.   **E5 33**
ST. ANNE & ST. AGNES,   **D3 32**
Gresham St.1677-80.
ST. BENET, Upper Thames St. 1677-83.   **D5 32**
Said to be the work of Robert Hooke, a junior that worked in Wren's office, it somewhat resembles a Dutch church.
CHRIST CHURCH, Newgate St. 1677-87.   **C3 32**
The stylish tower is all that remains.
ST. MARTIN, Ludgate Hill.1677-87.   **C4 32**
ST. PETER, Cornhill. 1677-87   **G4 33**
ST. CLEMENT DANES, Strand. 1680-2   **H4 31**
The Airforce church with a statue of the controversial Bomber Harris standing outside. James Gibbs, the architect of St. Martin-in-the-Fields and a great follower of Wren, finished the spire. He was also responsible for St. Mary-le-Strand (G4 31) which is now located on a traffic island.
ST. MARY, Abchurch Lane.1681-6.   **F4 33**
A ceiling painted by James Thornhill.
ST. MARY, Aldermary, Queen Victoria St.   **E4 33**
1681-1704. Re-interpreted Gothic-style church.
ST. JAMES, Piccadilly. (1682-84)   **B6 30**
Not on the site of an existing fire damaged building, but a new church for Wren. Famous today for free lunchtime concerts and the daily craft market.
ST. CLEMENT, Clements Lane. 1683-87   **F5 33**
ST. MARGARET, Eastcheap 1684-89   **G5 33**
ST. ANDREW, Queen Victoria St. 1685-95   **C4 32**
ST. MARGARET, Lothbury. 1686-90   **F3 33**
ST. MICHAEL, College Hill, 1686-94   **E5 33**
There were many other fine churches built by Wren that have now disappeared due to bombing in the Second World War. He lived on the south side of the Thames in Bankside opposite St. Paul's, in a house that still stands near the new Globe (D6 32).

GREENWICH

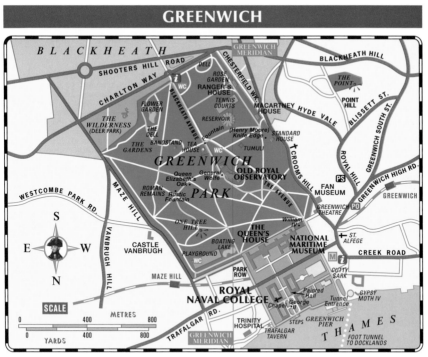

Greenwich is a marvel. It so close to Central London (four miles from Tower Bridge), yet it has the air of a picturesque fishing village. However, it also has probably the best Classical - Baroque display of architecture in the country, by some of England's greatest architects: Inigo Jones, Christopher Wren, John Webb and Nicholas Hawksmoor. The best way to reach Greenwich is by river boat: there are cruises from Westminster, Charing Cross and Tower Piers. Alternatively, the Docklands Light Railway will take you to Island Gardens where you can walk across under the Thames (lifts take you down to the tunnel). The atmospheric view of the Naval College from Island Gardens is incomparable, particularly on a nice evening. On Saturdays and Sundays there is a very good Arts and Crafts market (see map) in the historic covered market.

ROYAL NAVAL COLLEGE Originally built as a Hospital for sailors between 1664-1702. The West river fronting building was by John Webb, and then Wren produced the plan we now see, incorporating the original building into the grand plan.

The Painted Hall Arguably England's finest secular interior, designed by Nicholas Hawksmoor in the Baroque style, with marvellous paintings by James Thornhill, who painted the ceiling of St.Paul's. You can wheel a mirror trolley around to save craning your neck to view the painting - well worth seeing and it is free. It was here after Trafalgar that Nelson's body was brought to lie in state.

The Chapel was designed by Wren and Ripley and completed after Wren died. It is interesting to note that the two busts on each side of the door are of 'Kiss me' Hardy, a friend of Nelson and the poet Keats. Hardy was also a 'Shipmate' of the Sailor King, William IV!
Daily 14.30 - 16.45. *Free*

CUTTY SARK In a dry dock and now a museum, this ship broke records ploughing her way to and from China with cargoes of tea and wool.
April - September Monday - Saturday 10.00 - 18.00, Sunday 12.00 - 18.00, closed 17.00 Winter. Charge
GYPSY MOTH IV is the boat in which mapmaker, Francis Chichester, made the first round the world solo voyage in 1965-66.   *Small Charge*
THE NATIONAL MARITIME MUSEUM Very much devoted to Nelson and his historic achievements, there is a huge painting by Turner of the battle of Trafalgar. Of course that is not all: there are sections for Francis Drake, the practical Captain Cook and for John Franklin, whose name is recorded on maps of North America for posterity, reminding us of his relentless voyages to find the Northwest Passage.
The Queen's House A 17th century Palladian style villa by Inigo Jones that preceded everything else on the site. The wings were added after Trafalgar. The 'Tulip Staircase' is the star feature of the house.
Daily 10.00 - 17.00. *Free*
ST. ALFEGE This is a church by Hawksmoor. Like a temple in concept. General Wolfe was buried here.
OLD ROYAL OBSERVATORY Built by Christopher Wren, it now houses the Museum of Astronomy. To the left of the gates is the Meridian Building, which since 1884 has been the starting point of global measurement for time and space - the 'Prime Meridian' - check your watch here!
Daily 10.00 - 17.00. *Charge*
GREENWICH PARK Open from dawn until dusk, and originally laid out by Le Nôtre, of Versailles fame. The park is full of interest: a magnificent statue of General Wolfe at the top of the hill (a great place to take photos), Henry Moore sculpture, the remains of a Roman Temple, and a Deer Park are just a few of the features to look out for.

SERVICES AND USEFUL INFORMATION

Information Centres

| ☎ | Prefix numbers with 020 when dialling from outside CENTRAL LONDON |

BRITAIN VISITOR CENTRE   C6 30
1 Regent Street, Piccadilly Circus, SW1Y 4NS.

LONDON TOURIST BOARD
Telephone Information Service   ☎ *0839 123 456*
Tourist Information Centres
Victoria Station, SW1.
8.00 - 19.00 Daily, Sunday 18.00.
Liverpool St. Underground Station, EC2M 7PN.
8.00-1800 Daily, Saturday & Sunday 8.30 - 18.00.
Waterloo International Terminal, SE1 7LT.
Daily 8.30 - 22.30.
City of London Information Centre
St.Paul's Churchyard, EC4   ☎ *020 7332 1456*

AIR TRAVEL
GATWICK *(flight enquiries)* ☎ *0870 000 2468*
HEATHROW   ☎ *0870 000 0123*
LUTON   ☎ *01582 405 100*
STANSTED   ☎ *0870 0000 303*
LONDON CITY   ☎ *020 7646 0000*

BRITISH AIRWAYS
156 Regent Street, SW1   ☎ *020 7434 4700*
BRITISH AIRWAYS CHECK IN TERMINAL at
Paddington Station, W2   ☎ *0845 779 9977*

WEATHER FORECAST   ☎ *0906 850 0401*

DOCKLANDS LIGHT RAILWAY
Docklands Travel Hotline ☎ *020 7918 4000*
Travel Check   ☎ *020 7222 1200*

Emergency Services

AMBULANCE, FIRE, POLICE   ☎ *Dial 999*
MEDICAL SERVICE
Middlesex Hospital
Mortimer Street, W1
University College Hospital
Gower Street, W1
DENTAL SERVICE
Eastman Dental Hospital
256 Gray's Inn Road, WC1X
Mondays to Fridays 09.00 - 16.00
Outside these hours go to a General Hospital.
EYE TREATMENT
Moorfields Eye Hospital
City Road, EC1
TRAFALGAR SQUARE POST OFFICE
William V Street, Trafalgar Square, WC2. P0
Mondays to Saturdays 08.00 - 20.00
LOST PROPERTY
For property lost in taxis or on the street apply to
any Police Station.
In taxis only, apply: 15 Penton Street, N1.
In Underground trains and buses apply
Lost Property Office: 200 Baker Street, NW1.
In Main Line Trains, contact the station master at
departure or destination stations.
In Department Stores, Hotels, Airports contact the
premises in question.
LATE OPENING CHEMISTS
Chemists in London districts work on a rotating
system for late opening. The lists are always
posted on the door or window. Otherwise the
local Police Station will have the information.

AIRPORT TRANSFER
Heathrow The Piccadilly Underground Station
at Heathrow takes you into the centre of London.
The Heathrow Express runs every 15 minutes
from Paddington Station (full check-in facility for
20 airlines) taking 20 minutes. ☎ *0845 600 1515*
Airbus 2 Heathrow Shuttle (see Page 17): from
all terminals commencing at terminal 4 with four
departures an hour, 18 stops in Central London
finishing at Kings Cross Station.
Gatwick The Gatwick Express runs to and from
Victoria Station 04.30-06.00 and 20.00-00.30
every 30 minutes, from 06.00-20.00 it runs every
15 minutes. Allow approximately 35 minutes for
the journey   ☎ *0845 850 1530*
Stansted The Stansted Express operates to and
from Liverpool Street Station, the journey time is
approx. 40 minutes   ☎ *0845 850 0150*
An Airbus operates to and from the airport to
Victoria Coach Station.
BANKING HOURS
Banking hours are from 09.30-15.30 (although
many now stay open until 16.30) Mondays to
Fridays and with one exception all banks close on
Saturdays and Sundays. However some of the
larger department stores have banks and these
remain open during trading hours. Most banks
have cash machines outside available at all hours.
CREDIT CARDS
Most large shops, department stores, hotels and
restaurants will accept international credit cards
such as American Express, Diners' Club, Access
and Eurocard etc.
PUBLIC HOLIDAYS
New Years Day January 1st
Good Friday (late March early April)
May Day (the first Monday)
Spring Bank Holiday last Monday in May
Summer Bank Holiday last Monday in August
Christmas Day December 25th
Boxing Day December 26th
INTERNATIONAL TELEPHONE CALLS
To make an international call dial 00 then dial the
Country Code followed by the individual number.
To make a call to London from outside the United
Kingdom dial the international code then 44.
TELEPHONE DIRECTORY ENQUIRIES
118 500 for numbers in the United Kingdom.
118 505 for International Numbers.
From a Public Call Box this service is free

CLOTHING and SHOE SIZES approximate						
SHIRTS						
Europe	36	37	38	39	40	41	42
UK and USA	14	14.5	15	15.5	16	16.5	17
DRESSES						
Europe	36	38	40	42	44	46	48
UK	8	10	12	14	16	18	20
USA	6	8	10	12	14	16	18
MEN'S SHOES						
Europe	39	40	41	42	43	44	45
UK and USA	6	7	7.5	8.5	9	10	11
WOMEN'S SHOES						
Europe	35.5	36	36.5	37	37.5	38	39
UK	3	3.5	4	4.5	5	5.5	6
USA	4.5	5	5.5	6	6.5	7	7.5

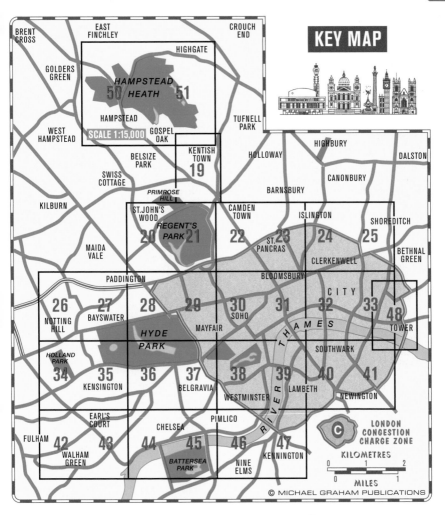

KEY MAP

© MICHAEL GRAHAM PUBLICATIONS

1:10,000   approximately 6 inches to 1 mile
1 CENTIMETRE TO 100 METRES   **SCALE**

300 METRES EQUAL 328 YARDS

METRES

0   100   200   300

ENGLISH   The maps are divided into 300 metre squares with divisions of 100 metres indicated in the border.

FRANÇAIS   Les cartes sont divisées en carrés de 300 mètres de côté, avec divisions de 100 mètres indiquées en bordure.

DEUTSCH   Die karten sind in karrees von 300 quadratmeter unterteilt 100-Meter-Unterteilung ist am Rand markiert.

NEDERLANDS   De kaarten zijn verdeeld in vierkanten van 300 meter met verdelingen van 100 meter in de kantlijn.

ITALIANO   Le mappe sono suddivise in 300 metri quadrati con divisione di 100 metri indicate nel margine.

ESPAÑOL   Las cartas están divididas en cuadrados de 300 metros, con divisiones de 100 metros indicados en el margen.

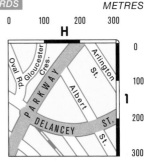

LEGEND - ENGLISH - FRANÇAIS - DEUTSCH - NEDERLANDS - ITALIANO - ESPAÑOL

HOSPITALS
Hôpitaux
Krankenhäus
Ziekenhuisen
Ospedali
Hospitales

St.Mary's
Hospital

TOURIST INFORMATION
Informations Touristiques
Touristenauskünfte
Toeristen Informatie
Informazione Turistiche
Información Turistica

POLICE STATION
Gendarmerie
Polizeiwache
Politie
Polizia
Comisaría

PS

FOOTPATH
Sentier
Fusspfad
Voetpad
Sentiero
Senda

POST OFFICE
Bureau de Poste
Postamt
Postkantoor
Ufficio Postale
Correos

PO

PUBLIC PARK
Jardin Public
Öffentliche Parkanlage
Publiek Park
Giardino Pubblico
Parque Publico

PHARMACY
Pharmacie
Apotheke
Apotheek
Farmacia
Farmácia

CEMETERY
Cimetière
Friedhof
Begraafplaats
Cimiteri
Cementerio

HOTEL
Hôtel
Hotel
Hotel
Albergo
Hotel

DORCHESTER

OUTDOOR STATUES and SCULPTURES
Statues et Sculptures dehors
Im Freien stehende Standbilder und Skulpturen
Standbeelden en Beeldhouwkunst buiten
Statue e Sculture all'aperto
Estatura y Escultura al fresco

Edith Cavell

CHURCHES
Églises
Kirchen
Kirken
Chiese di
Iglesias

St. Helen's †

THEATRES and CONCERT HALLS
Théâtres et Salles de Concerts
Theater und Konzertsäle
Theaters en Concertzalen
Teatri e Sale dei Concerti
Teatros y Salas de Concertos

COLISEUM ■

SYNAGOGUE
Synagogue
Synagoge
Synagogen
Sinagoga
Sinagoga

✡

CINEMA
Cinéma
Kino
Bioscoop
Cinema
Cine

EMPIRE ■

JAZZ CLUB
Jazz Club
Jazz Club
Jazz Club
Jazz Club
Jazz Club

RONNIE ★
SCOTT'S

RESTAURANT OR CAFE
Restaurant ou Café
Restaurant oder Cafe
Restaurant of Café
Ristorante o Cafe
Restorant o Cafe

Le Tour de la Pont ●

DISCO or DANCE HALL
Disco ou Salle de Danse
Disko oder Tanzsaal
Disco of Dans Zaal
Disco o Sala di Danza
Disco o Salón de Baile

The Forum ★

PUBLIC HOUSE
Pub
Ausschank
Herberg
Taverna
Taberna

The Spaniards ★
Inn

BUS ROUTE TERMINUS
Terminus d'Autobus
Endstation, Autobuslinie
Autobuslijn Eindpunt
Capolinea Autobus
Terminus de Linea Autobus

34

RAILWAY STATION
Gares
Bahnhof
Station
Stazione
Estación

**(EASTERN REGION)
LIVERPOOL
STREET**

WC **TOILET** Toilette Toilet Toeletta Retrete

UNDERGROUND SYSTEM

MARBLE ARCH The COLOURS of the Station Name Boxes indicate the Underground Lines that stop at the Station. *(Thus Marble Arch is on the Central Line)*

LE METRO
LONDONIEN

La COULEUR de la case portant le nom de la station indique la ligne qui la dessert. *(Example: la station Marble Arch est située sur la ligne Central)*

U-BAHN-NETZ

Di FARBEN der Station - Namenschilder deuten auf die U-Bahn-Linien, die Stationen bedienen. *(Die Marble-Arch-Station liegt also auf der Central-Linie)*

DE ONDERGRONDSE

De KLEUREN van de stationnamen geven de verschillende lijnen aan die op dat station stoppen. *(Dus Marble Arch Station ligt op de Central lijn)*

LA METROPOLITANA

Il nome della stazione é dimostrato in COLORI rappresentativi delle differenti linee. *(Quindi la Stazione di Marble Arch si trova sulla linea Central)*

EL METRO

La estaciones del Metro se indican en COLORES que representan las lineas. *(La Estación de Marble Arch está en la linea CENTRAL)*

UNDERGROUND LINE COLOURS

BAKERLOO	CENTRAL	CIRCLE	DISTRICT	NORTHERN

JUBILEE	VICTORIA	PICCADILLY	METROPOLITAN	WATERLOO & CITY	HAMMERSMITH & CITY

AIRBUSES - AÉROBUS - FLUGHAFENBUSVERBINDUNG - LUCHTBUS - AEROBUS - AEROBUS

AIRBUS A2 Heathrow Airport - Kings Cross Station 　**AIRBUS A6** Stansted Airport - Victoria Coach Station

A2 STOPS - Arrêt - Haltestellen - Stoppen - Fermata - Parada

STATION LINK SERVICES

Paddington • Marylebone • Warren St. • Euston • Kings Cross/St.Pancras • Islington • Old Street • Moorgate • Liverpool St. • Aldgate • Whitechapel Road • Whitechapel Station 　**205**

Paddington • Victoria Coach Station • Victoria • St.Thomas' Hospital • Waterloo • London Bridge • Fenchurch Street • Liverpool Street 　**705**

DAY BUS ROUTES WITH NUMBERS
Ligne d'autobus quotidienne avec numéros - Busstrecke tagsüber mit linien-nummern
Dagelijkse Autobuslijn met Nummers - Autobus quotidiano con Numeri
La Ruta de Autobuses durante dia con Números

BUS ROUTES in GREY
Arrows indicate BUSES in one direction only.

Lignes d'autobus en GRIS. *Les flèches indiquent les lignes d'autobus dans un seul sens.*

GRAUE busstrecken.
Pfeile zeigen auf Busverkehr nur in Pfeil-richtung.

Autobuslijnen in GRIJS.
Pijlen geven de bussen aan alleen in één direktie.

Linee di Autobus in GRIGIO.
Le frecce indicano autobus in una sola direzione.

Ruta autobús en GRIS.
Las flechas indican la ruta de los autobuses en una sola dirección.

BUS ROUTE NUMBERS are indicated in the border.

Les lignes dépassant les bordures de la carte sont indiquées en marge.

Buslinien-Nummern sind am Kartenrand angegeben.

Bus route nummers zijn aangegeven in de kantlijn.

I numeri delle linee di autobus son indicate sul margine.

Los números de autobús se indican en el margen.

PLACES OF INTEREST - ENDROITS INTERESSANTS - SEHENSWÜRDIGKEITEN - BEZIENSWAARDIGHEDEN - LUOGHI DI INTERESSE - LUGARES DE INTERES

IMPORTANT BUILDINGS
Bâtiments importants
Wichtige Gebäude
Belangrijke gebouwen
Edifici importanti
Edifícios importantes

BANK OF ENGLAND

BUILDINGS open to the PUBLIC
Edifices ouverts au public
Allgemein zugängliche Gebäude
Gebouwen met toegang voor het publiek
Edifici aperti al pubblico
Edificios abiertos al público

ST.PAUL'S CATHEDRAL

SHOPPING - MAGASINS - EINKÄUFE - WINKELEN - ACQUISTI - COMPRAS

A SELECTION OF SHOPS - Choix de Magasins - Einige Läden - Keus van Winkels - Scelta di Negozi - Selección de Tiendas

LIBERTY

STREET MARKETS - Marché en plein air - Straßenmarkt - Straatmarkt
Mercato all'aperto - Mercado callejero

SHOPPING

People come from all over the world just to shop in London and justifiably so, with two of the world's most celebrated department stores - Harrod's and Selfridges - and all kinds of shops and markets for any size of pocket.

Shopping Areas

BOND STREET   A5 30
Divided in two sections - Old Bond Street and New Bond street. A street of fashionable shops and fine art dealers, with many respected names in fashion. Fenwick's department store, Chappell's music shop, and the home of Sotheby's the auctioneers.

BURLINGTON ARCADE   B6 30
Running into Piccadilly and patrolled by uniformed beadles, it is very expensive but exquisite! Elegant specialist shops sell, silver, jewellery and knitwear.

CARNABY STREET   B4 30
Associated with the Pop Culture and fashion of the 60s this colourful street became a legend. Today it still retains a unique atmosphere.

CHARING CROSS ROAD   D3 30
A road that never ceases to attract scholars and musicians. Many bookshops headed by the unique Foyles in two buildings, with over four million books on sale. Music shops are on this street and in side turnings like Denmark Street.

JERMYN STREET   B6 30
If you need shirts here is the place to have them made to measure. Expensive jewellery shops are here too with a perfumiers and a specialist cheesemonger.

KENSINGTON HIGH STREET   D4 34
A popular shopping street for young fashions, boutiques and high-class couture, landmarked by the 1938 modernity of Barkers department store - now franchised to House of Fraser and others.

KINGS ROAD, CHELSEA   B3 44
Boutiques, pubs, bistros, antique dealers, and one department store on Sloane Square called Peter Jones (a John Lewis store). On summer Saturdays the road becomes one long art gallery where anyone can display their paintings.

KNIGHTSBRIDGE   D3 36
Unequalled for its fashion, food and art shops. This is where to find Harrods and what was Lady Diana's favourite store, Harvey Nichols.

NEAL STREET   E4 31
A relatively new thriving shopping area for young people close to Covent Garden piazza.

OXFORD STREET   F4 29
London's most famous shopping street with large department stores including Selfridges, Marks & Spencer, D. H.Evans, and Debenhams etc. HMV has two shops for CDs and records - the eastern one is the largest - see also the Virgin store.

REGENT STREET   B4 30
This gently curving street of noble architecture is where to find the immutable yet changing department store Liberty's and the largest toy shop in Europe, Hamley's. Disney and Warner Brothers have also congregated alongside.

TOTTENHAM COURT ROAD   C1 30
Apart from the great furnishing shop Heal's, this is the home of bargain HiFi; TV; Radio; Computers and almost anything electronic. Check around before you buy and you should get a good bargain!

> **TRADING TIMES** *Shops usually open at 9.00 and close at 17.30 Monday to Saturday, closing at 19.00 on Thursdays in the West End, Wednesdays in Knightsbridge, Sloane Square and Kings Road.*

Department Stores

DICKINS & JONES   A4 30
Near the Palladium, this is a nice store for male and female fashion, with plenty of room to browse.

FORTNUM & MASON   B6 30
Respected for its provisions department, tea, coffee, jams and aristocratic sales persona etc.

HARRODS   D4 36
Above all else, do not miss the Edwardian food hall; it is out of this world, undeniably one of the world's greatest stores. See the fountain memorial to Princess Diana and Dodi Fayed on the lower ground floor.

HARVEY NICHOLS   E3 37
Stylish and well known for vogueish fashion with a very good food hall on the top floor.

JOHN LEWIS   H3 29
The Oxford Street branch is the flagship of this standardised chain. Good quality products but not as interesting as some of the other stores here.

LIBERTY   B4 30
Famous for its amazing 1924 Tudor-style building and its classic fabrics. Children will enjoy the clock outside - St.George chases the dragon every 15 mins.

SELFRIDGES   F4 29
Spacious and renowned for its sales, the interior has recently been renovated. Above the main entrance is a superb Art-deco clock. Everything you need can be bought here. Delicious tea in the restaurants when you want to rest your feet.

Markets

BERWICK STREET   C4 30
Soho's busy friendly fruit & vegetable market Monday to Saturday from 5.00.

BRICK LANE   D1 48
London's curry centre, and heart of the leather industry, odds and ends etc. Sunday mornings.

BRIXTON Off the map area in an arcade and streets near the station. Worth a visit for the exotic sunny caribbean atmosphere - absolutely marvellous for fish. Monday to Saturday. Underground Brixton.

CAMDEN PASSAGE   B2 24
Small Islington outdoor antique market, Weds & Sats.

CAMDEN MARKETS   C5 19
A daily indoor market, arts, crafts, clothes etc. The outdoor market is a tourist attraction and is open from Thursday to Sunday.

CHURCH STREET   B1 28
General market, good for antiques. Mons- Sats.

COVENT GARDEN   F5 31
A covered market with buskers outside in the piazza to entertain you. Monday antiques, and Tuesday to Sunday arts and crafts 9.00 - 16.00.

LEADENHALL   A3 48
Classic indoor market, incorporates the famous Lamb Tavern. Meat, poultry, fish, plants. Mons - Fris.

LEATHER LANE   A2 32
Lunchtime market Monday to Friday.

NEW CALEDONIAN   H3 41
Quality antiques, go early. Mons - Fris 6.00 - 14.00.

PETTICOAT LANE   B1 48
Famous and large street market.   Sundays am.

PORTOBELLO ROAD   B4 26
Boutiques, antiques, almost anything. Mons - Sats.

SPITALFIELDS   C1 48
Antiques and crafts weekdays 9.00 - 17.00, Fridays and Sundays organic market.

KENTISH TOWN

MAITLAND PARK

CHALK FARM

KENTISH TOWN WEST

PRINCE OF WALES

PRIMROSE HILL

CAMDEN TOWN

LORD'S CRICKET GROUND
THE MECCA OF CRICKET

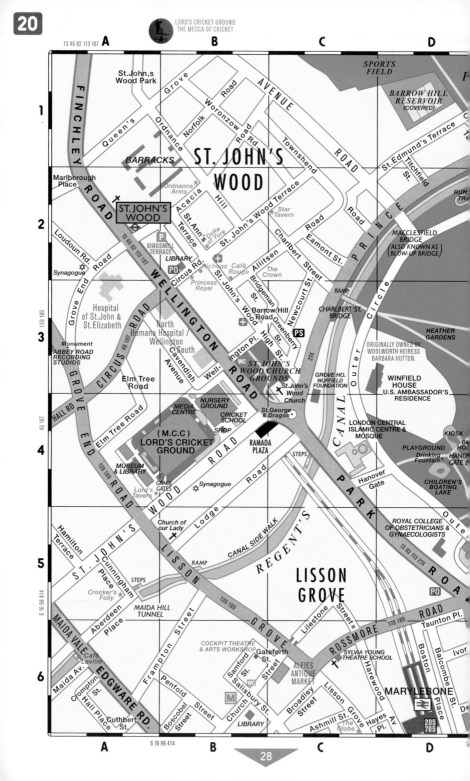

A · B · C · D

SPORTS FIELD

BARROW HILL RESERVOIR (COVERED)

St.John,s Wood Park

Grove

Woronzow Road

Norfolk Road

Road

AVENUE

Townshend

St.Edmund's Terrace

Titchfield St.

RUN TRA

1

Marlborough Place

Queen's

Ordnance

ST. JOHN'S WOOD

ROAD

PRINCE

2

BARRACKS

Acacia

Hill

Road

MACCLESFIELD BRIDGE (ALSO KNOWN AS BLOW-UP BRIDGE)

ST. JOHN'S WOOD

Ordnance Arms

St.John's Wood Terrace

Star Tavern

Charlbert Street

Eamont St.

Road

St.Ann's Terrace

Duke of York

Loudoun Rd.

Road

KINGSMILL TERRACE

LIBRARY

Circus Rd.

Nicholas

Café Rouge

Allitsen

The Crown

Synagogue

PO

Princess Royal

St. John's Wood

Bridgeman St.

Greenberry St.

Newcourt St.

CHARLBERT ST. BRIDGE

RAMP

HEATHER GARDENS

Grove End Road

Hospital of St.John & St.Elizabeth

North Humana Hospital / Wellington

Barrow Hill Road

High St.

PS

ORIGINALLY OWNED BY WOOLWORTH HEIRESS BARBARA HUTTON.

3

139 189

Monument ABBEY ROAD RECORDING STUDIOS

CIRCUS

South Cavendish Avenue

Wellington Pl.

274

GROVE HO. NUFFIELD FOUNDATION

Outer Circle

WINFIELD HOUSE U.S. AMBASSADOR'S RESIDENCE

46 187

HALL RD

Elm Tree Road

ROAD

WELLINGTON

Well-

WC

ST. JOHN'S WOOD CHURCH GROUNDS

St.John's Wood Church

CANAL

LONDON CENTRAL ISLAMIC CENTRE & MOSQUE

KIOSK

BO

4

MEDIA CENTRE

NURSERY GROUND

CRICKET SCHOOL

SHOP

St.George & Dragon

PLAYGROUND

HANO

GATE B

(M.C.C) LORD'S CRICKET GROUND

RAMADA PLAZA

STEPS

Drinking Fountain

PARK

CHILDREN'S BOATING LAKE

MUSEUM & LIBRARY

GRACE GATES

ROAD

Synagogue

Hanover Gate

139 189

Lord's Tavern

Lodge

ROYAL COLLEGE OF OBSTETRICIANS & GYNAECOLOGISTS

5

Hamilton Terrace

ROAD

Church of our Lady

Road

CANAL SIDE WALK

REGENT'S

13 82 113 274

Outer

ST. JOHN'S

Cunningham Place

RAMP

LISSON

LISSON GROVE

ROAD

6 16 98 414

Crocker's Folly

STEPS

Frampton Street

139 189

Lilestone Street

Street

PO

MAIDA VALE

Aberdeen Place

MAIDA HILL TUNNEL

GROVE

ROSSMORE

Taunton Pl.

Boston

Balcombe Pl.

Ivor

6

Café Laville

Maida Av.

Crompton St.

Hall Place

EDGWARE RD.

Cuthbert St.

Penfold Street

Boscobel Street

Church Street

COCKPIT THEATRE & ARTS WORKSHOP

Gateforth St.

Samford St.

Salisbury St.

WC

M

LIBRARY

Gateforth Street

ALFIES ANTIQUE MARKET

Broadley Street

SYLVIA YOUNG THEATRE SCHOOL

Lisson Grove

Harewood

Ashmill St.

Hayes Pl.

Hayes Av

The Globe

MARYLEBONE

205 705

A · B · C · D

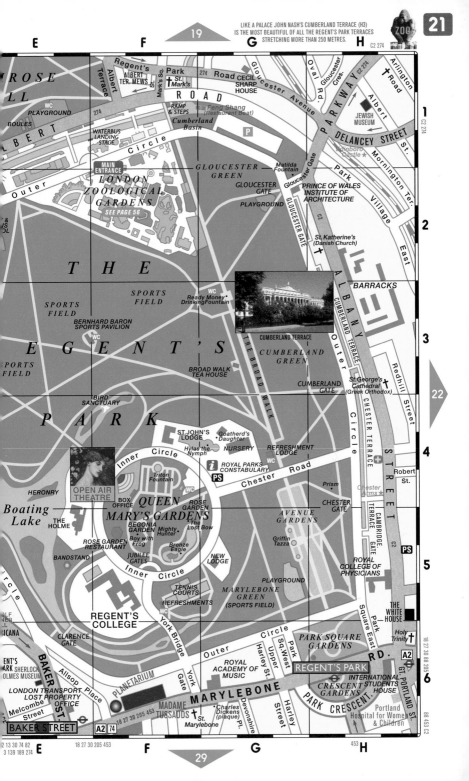

E   F   19   G   H   21

LIKE A PALACE JOHN NASH'S CUMBERLAND TERRACE (H3)
IS THE MOST BEAUTIFUL OF ALL THE REGENT'S PARK TERRACES
STRETCHING MORE THAN 250 METRES.
C2 274

ZOO

Regent's
Park
PLAYGROUND
BOULES
WC
ALBERT
ROSE
LL
Albert
Terrace
REGENT'S
TER. MEWS
St Mark's Sq.
St.
Mark's
Road
274
ROAD
Gloucester Avenue
Gloucester
Cres.
Oval
Gloucester
Rd.
PARKWAY
C2 274
Arlington
Road
Jewish
Museum
Albert
Street
1
C2 274

RAMP
& STEPS
Cumberland
Basin
Feng Shang
(Restaurant Boat)
WATERBUS
LANDING
STAGE
P
Circle
274
Gloucester Gate
DELANCEY STREET
Edinboro
Castle ★
Mornington Ter.
St.
ALBERT

MAIN
ENTRANCE
Outer
GLOUCESTER
GREEN
Matilda
Fountain
Park
Prince Village
GLOUCESTER
GATE
PRINCE OF WALES
INSTITUTE OF
ARCHITECTURE
LONDON
ZOOLOGICAL
GARDENS
SEE PAGE 56
PLAYGROUND
GLOUCESTER GATE
C2
East
2
& JS
OL

THE
SPORTS
FIELD
SPORTS
FIELD
BERNHARD BARON
SPORTS PAVILION
WC
Ready Money
Drinking Fountain
St. Katherine's
(Danish Church)
BARRACKS
ALBANY
CUMBERLAND TERRACE

CUMBERLAND TERRACE
3
REGENT'S

SPORTS
FIELD
THE BROAD WALK
CUMBERLAND
GREEN
BIRD
SANCTUARY
BROAD WALK
TEA HOUSE
CUMBERLAND
GATE
Outer
St. George's
Cathedral
(Greek Orthodox)
Redhill
Street
Circle
22

PARK
ST. JOHN'S
LODGE
Goatherd's
Daughter
Hylas the
Nymph
Triton
Fountain
NURSERY
REFRESHMENT
LODGE
WC
ROYAL PARKS
CONSTABULARY
i
PS
Chester
Road
Prism
Chester
Arms ★
CHESTER TERRACE
Robert
St.
4
HERONRY
OPEN AIR
THEATRE
Inner
Circle
BOX
OFFICE
QUEEN
MARY'S GARDENS
WC
ROSE
GARDEN
The
Lost Bow
AVENUE
GARDENS
CHESTER
GATE
St
CAMBRIDGE
TERRACE
Boating
Lake
THE
HOLME
BEGONIA
GARDEN
Boy with
Frog
Mighty
Hunter
Bronze
Eagle
Griffin
Tazza
CAMBRIDGE
GATE
C2
ROSE GARDEN
RESTAURANT
JUBILEE
GATES
NEW
LODGE
ROYAL
COLLEGE OF
PHYSICIANS
PS
BANDSTAND
Inner
Circle
PLAYGROUND
5
cle
OLF
LL
ICANA
TENNIS
COURTS
REFRESHMENTS
MARYLEBONE
GREEN
(SPORTS FIELD)
THE
WHITE
HOUSE
REGENT'S
COLLEGE
WC
Circle
PARK SQUARE
GARDENS
Holy
Trinity
18 27 30 88 205
CLARENCE
GATE
York Bridge
Park
Square East
ENT'S
ARK
SHERLOCK
OLMES MUSEUM
Allsop Place
Outer
Circle
Park
Sq. West
Upper
Harley St.
Park
Street
RD.
A2
REGENT'S PARK
88 453 C2

BAKER
ST.
York
Gate
ROYAL
ACADEMY
OF
MUSIC
Harley
Street
INTERNATIONAL
STUDENTS
HOUSE
GT. PORTLAND ST.
6
LONDON TRANSPORT
LOST PROPERTY
OFFICE
Melcombe
Street
PLANETARIUM
MARYLEBONE
MADAME
TUSSAUDS
St.
Marylebone
Charles
Dickens
(plaque)
Devonshire
Pl.
CRESCENT
GARDENS
PARK CRESCENT
Portland
Hospital for Women
& Children

BAKER STREET
A2   74
2 13 30 74 82
3 139 189 274
E
18 27 30 205 453
F
29
G
453
H

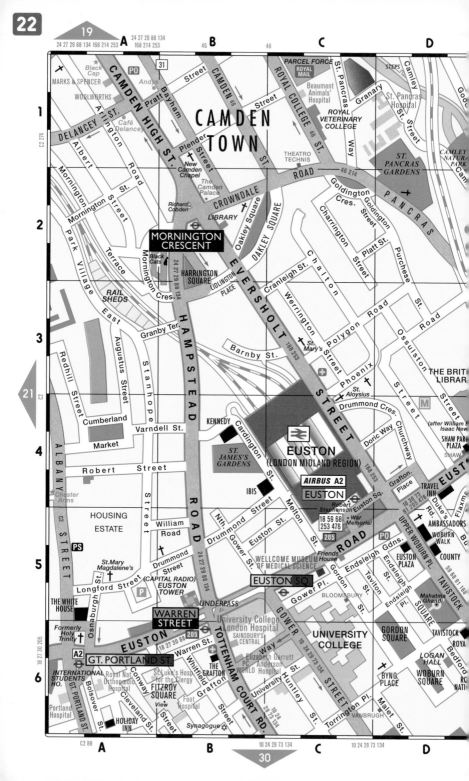

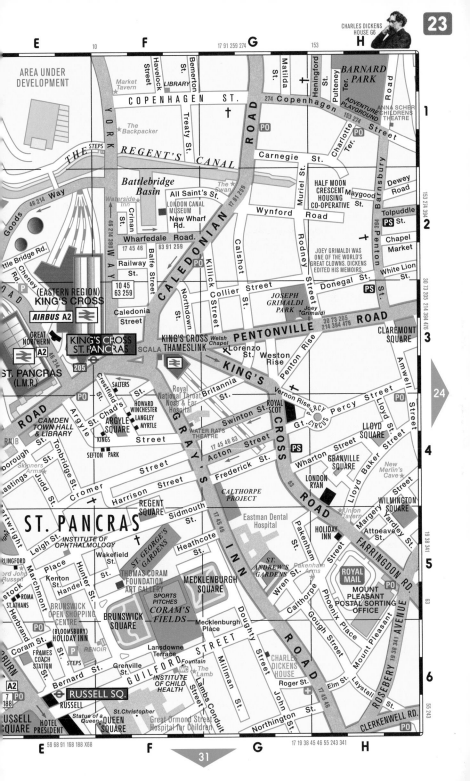

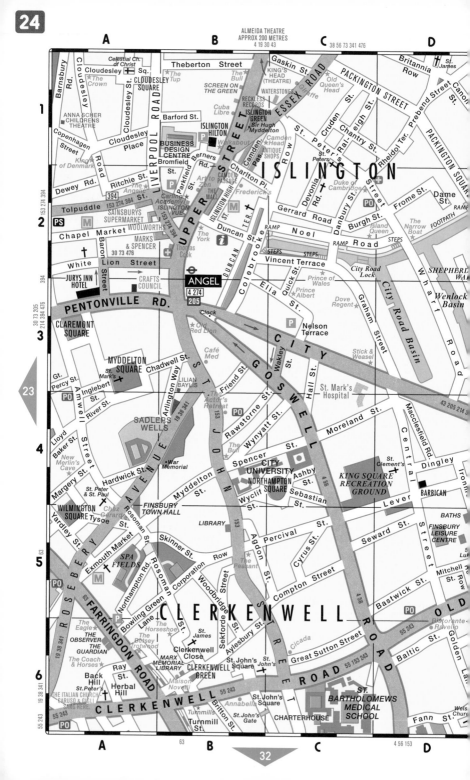

SITE OF GAINSBOROUGH STUDIOS
ALFRED HITCHCOCK FILMED
'THE LADY VANISHES' HERE

E 271   F 76 141   G   H

(Grand Union Canal)

Kingsland
Basin

1

Street
Street

ARLINGTON
SQUARE

Arlington Avenue

Sturt's
Lock

Eagle Wharf Road

REGENT'S

CANAL

NEW

NORTH

ROAD

STEPS

Baring Street

STEPS

Poole Street

Bridport Place

Penn Street

Northport

Gopsall St.

SCHOOL

BRITANNIA
LEISURE
CENTRE

Hyde Rd.

Whitmore Rd.

Orsman   Road

Phillipp   Street

King's
Arms

St.
Anne's

Nuttall St.

The
Unicorn

394

1

SHOREDITCH
PARK

SPORTS
PITCHES

TENNIS
COURTS

Street

Hemsworth St.

Hoxton

ST. LEONARD'S
COMMUNITY
SERVICES

394

2

Forston St.

Cropley

Street

Wimbourne St.

394

Mintern   Street

HOXTON
CENTRE
(Salvation Army)

Ivy Street

Purcell

St.

Regan Way

Stanway

St.

GEFFRYE
MUSEUM

67 149 242 243 394

2

SHEPHERDESS

Wenlock

394

Street

Evelyn
Walk

Holy Trinity

Murray 394

Grove

PO

Provost

Buckland

St.

Cherbury

St.

St. John
the Baptist

Pitfield

Crondall St.

THE
LION CLUB
(for young people)

Shenfield

St.

Falkirk St.

394

PO

3

WALK

WELLESLEY TER.

394

William
IV
St.

Nile

Street

Bevenden   Street

St.

NEW NORTH ROAD

76 141 271

Fanshaw

St.

SHOREDITCH

St.
Monica's
(Catholic)

Street

3

ROAD

PS
The
Eagle

Mora
Street

43 205 214

INSTITUTE OF
OPHTHALMOLOGY

Cayton St.

Peerless St.

Provost St.

VESTRY ST.

Haberdasher

WHARFSIDE

Chart St.

Buttesland

St.

Chart St.

Bowling
Green Walk

THE
CIRCUS
SPACE

Coronet

Mundy
St.

HOXTON
SQUARE

Drysdale

St.

DISSUSED RAILWAY LINE

KINGSLAND

Hackney Rd.

26 48 55

4

EAST

CITY

Moorfields
Eye Hospital

Brunswick Pla.

Cranwood

Vince

St.

CHARLES
SQUARE

EXPRESS
BY HOLIDAY INN

Juggling
Figure

Crosby
Head

43 55
243

Rivington

Charlotte Rd.

Curtain Road

Street

Bateman's

35 47 78

SHOREDITCH
TOWN HALL

Calvert
Av.

78

Row

New Inn

Yard

8 47 78

CALVERT

4

BATH

STREET

anor
St.

205

OLD

PO

OLD ST.

St. St.

Fountain

Tabernacle St.

OLD

GREAT

43

STREET

EASTERN

5

ROAD

55 243

Tanner St.

Street

Featherstone Rd.

Yeung's
City Bar

The
Angel

SHOREDITCH
COUNTY
COURT

Leonard

Street

Street

St.
Michael's

Luke

St.

Street

Phipp St.

Holywell

St.

SHOREDITCH

HIGH

PO

The
Bar

5

M

Whitecross

Street

Dufferin St.

St.
Joseph

CITY
UNIVERSITY

BUNHILL

ROW

BUNHILL
FIELDS
Daniel
De-Foe
BURIAL
GROUND

Artillery
Arms

William
Blake

John
Bunyan

HONOURABLE
ARTILLERY
COMPANY
H.Q.

NEW
ARTILLERY
GARDEN

WESLEY'S HO
& MUSEUM
John
Wesley

Wesley's
Chapel

P

Clere St.

Epworth St.

Tabernacle

P

Worship

St.

FINSBURY
SQUARE

Paul

Clifton

St.

Scrutton

Street

St.

Wilson

Clifton

Street

Curtain Road

The
Fox

St.

Worship

DISSUSED RAILWAY LINE

STREET

Worship St.

6

67

6

E   F 43 76 141 205 214 271 21 271 G   H 8 26 35 43 47
48 78 149 242

33

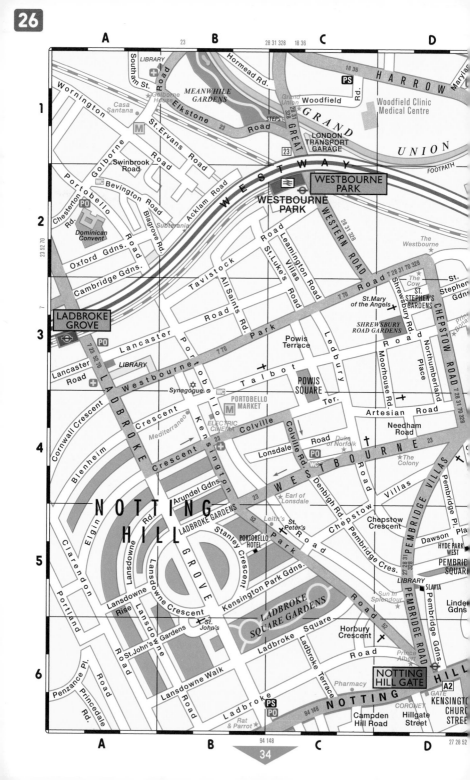

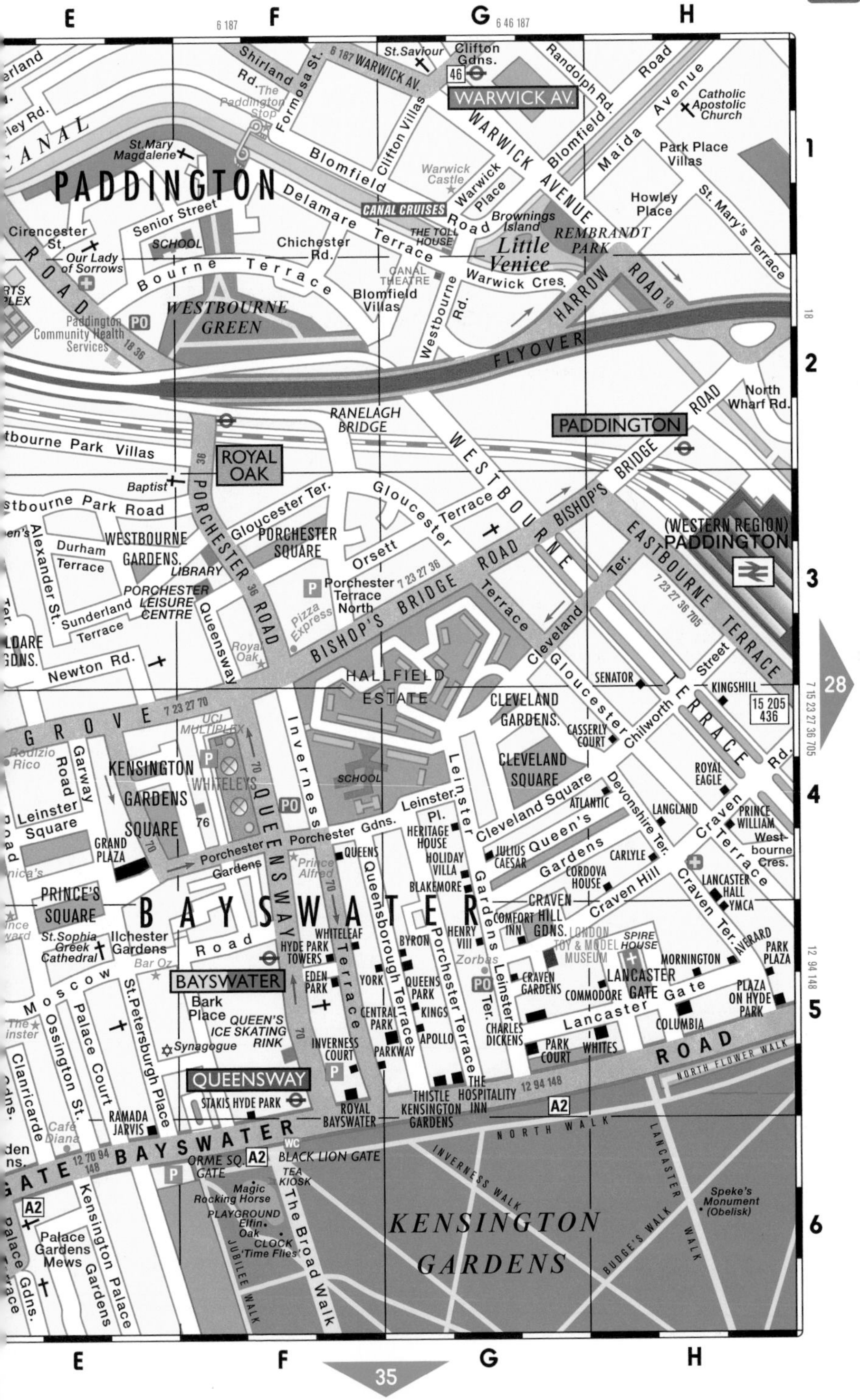
E
F
G
H
PADDINGTON
BAYSWATER
KENSINGTON GARDENS
Little Venice
WARWICK AV.
PADDINGTON
ROYAL OAK
BAYSWATER
QUEENSWAY
(WESTERN REGION) PADDINGTON
Shirland Rd.
Formosa St.
Warwick Av.
St.Saviour
Clifton Gdns.
Randolph Rd.
Maida Avenue
Catholic Apostolic Church
Park Place Villas
Howley Place
St. Mary's Terrace
Blomfield Rd.
Clifton Villas
Warwick Castle
Warwick Place
Warwick Avenue
Blomfield Rd.
Delamare Terrace
CANAL CRUISES
THE TOLL HOUSE
Brownings Island
REMBRANDT PARK
Canal
The Paddington Stop
St.Mary Magdalene
Cirencester St.
Senior Street
SCHOOL
Chichester Rd.
Our Lady of Sorrows
Harrow Road
Bourne Terrace
WESTBOURNE GREEN
CANAL THEATRE
Blomfield Villas
Westbourne Rd.
Warwick Cres.
Harrow Road
Flyover
Paddington Community Health Services
North Wharf Rd.
Ranelagh Bridge
Westbourne Terrace
Westbourne Park Villas
Westbourne Park Road
Baptist
Porchester Road
Gloucester Ter.
Gloucester Terrace
Bishop's Bridge Road
Eastbourne Terrace
Westbourne Gardens
Durham Terrace
Alexander St.
Porchester Square
Orsett Terrace
Porchester Terrace North
LIBRARY
Porchester Leisure Centre
Sunderland Terrace
Queensway
Royal Oak
Pizza Express
Cleveland Ter.
Hallfield Estate
Newton Rd.
Grove
UCI Multiplex
Rodizio Rico
Garway Road
Kensington Gardens Square
Whiteleys
Inverness Terrace
Leinster Gardens
Cleveland Gardens
Cleveland Square
Senator
Casserly Court
Chilworth Street
Kingshill
Gloucester Terrace
Devonshire Ter.
Royal Eagle
Langland
Craven Terrace
Prince William
Westbourne Cres.
Atlantic
Leinster Square
Grand Plaza
Porchester Gardens
Porchester Gdns.
Queens
Leinster Pl.
Heritage House
Holiday Villa
Blakemore
Prince Alfred
Queensborough Terrace
Julius Caesar
Queen's Gardens
Carlyle
Cordova House
Craven Hill
Lancaster Hall
YMCA
Craven Ter.
Prince's Square
Craven Hill Gdns.
Comfort Inn
London Toy & Model Museum
Spire House
St.Sophia Greek Cathedral
Ilchester Gardens
Moscow Road
Whiteleaf
Hyde Park Towers
Byron
Henry VIII
Porchester Terrace
Averard
Park Plaza
Mornington
Bar Oz
Eden Park
York
Queens Park
Kings
Zorbas
Craven Gardens
Commodore
Lancaster Gate
Plaza on Hyde Park
Ossington St.
Palace Court
St.Petersburgh Place
Bark Place
Queen's Ice Skating Rink
Central Park
Apollo
Leinster Ter.
Charles Dickens
Lancaster Gate
Columbia
Park Court
Whites
Synagogue
Inverness Court
Parkway
The Hospitality Inn
Thistle Kensington Gardens
Royal Bayswater
Stakis Hyde Park
Ramada Jarvis
Bayswater Road
North Flower Walk
Clanricarde Gdns.
Café Diana
A2
North Walk
Black Lion Gate
Orme Sq. Gate
Tea Kiosk
Inverness Walk
Lancaster Walk
Kensington Palace Gardens
Magic Rocking Horse
Playground
Elfin Oak
Clock 'Time Flies'
The Broad Walk
Jubilee Walk
Budge's Walk
Speke's Monument (Obelisk)
Palace Gardens Mews
1
2
3
4
5
6
28
35

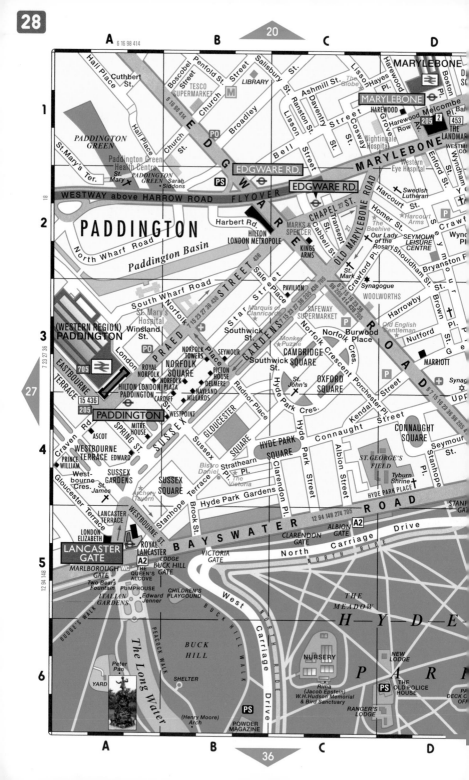

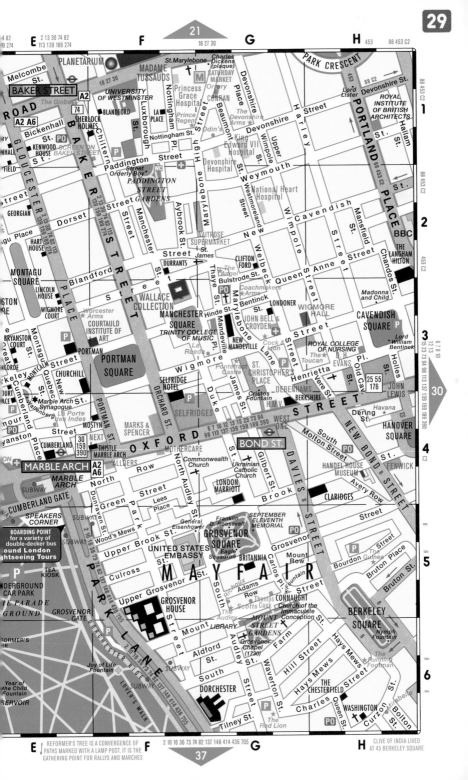

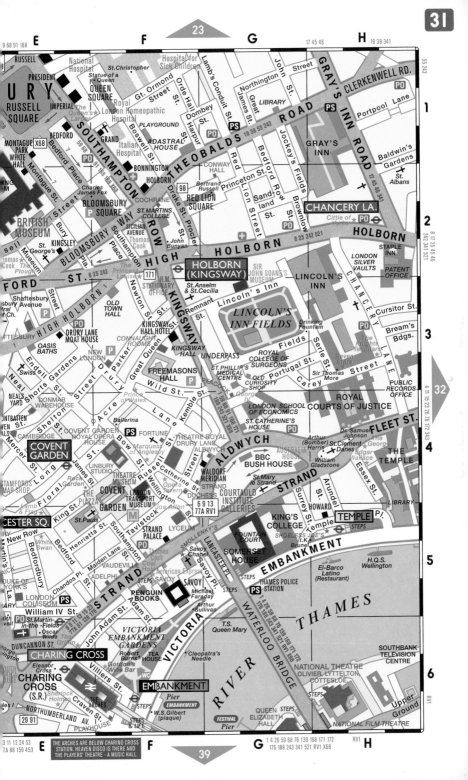

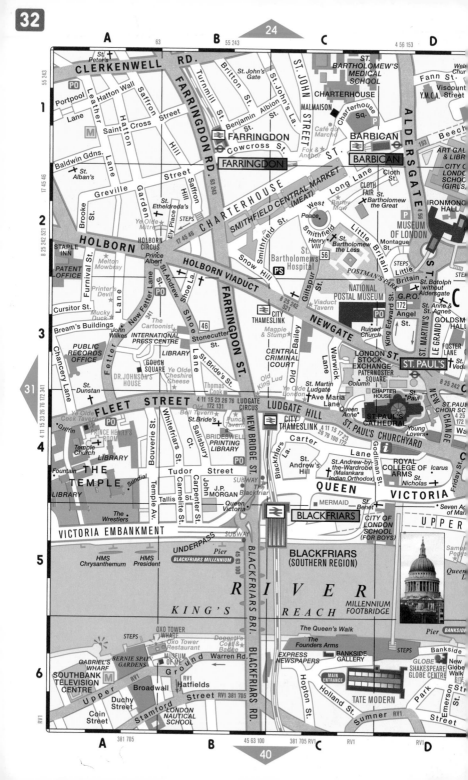

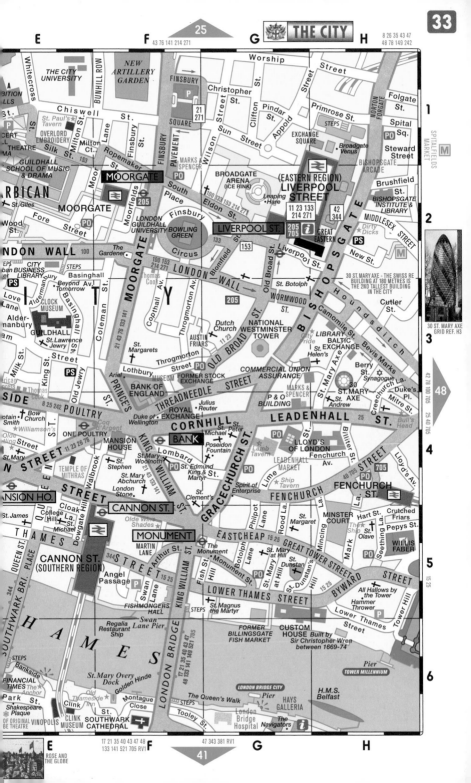

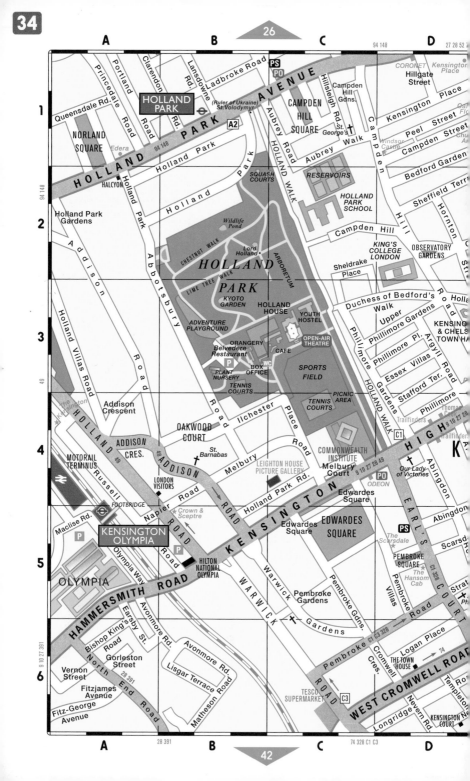

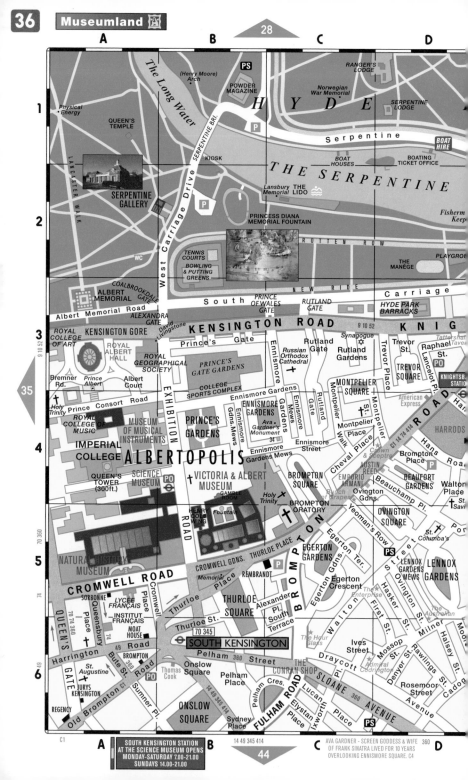

A   B   C   D

The Long Water

(Henry Moore) Arch

POWDER MAGAZINE

PS

RANGER'S LODGE

Norwegian War Memorial

SERPENTINE LODGE

H Y D E

Physical Energy

QUEEN'S Temple

1

Serpentine BRI.

KIOSK

P

Serpentine

BOAT HOUSES

BOATING TICKET OFFICE

BOAT HIRE

THE SERPENTINE

LANCASTER WALK

SERPENTINE GALLERY

West Carriage Drive

P

Lansbury Memorial

THE LIDO

PRINCESS DIANA MEMORIAL FOUNTAIN

R O T T E N   R O W

Fisherman Keep

PLAYGROU

THE MANÈGE

2

WC

TENNIS COURTS

BOWLING & PUTTING GREENS

COALBROOKDALE GATE

ALBERT MEMORIAL

ALEXANDRA GATE

South

PRINCE OF WALES GATE

RUTLAND GATE

NEW RIDE

HYDE PARK BARRACKS

Carriage

Albert Memorial Road

David Livingstone

9 10 52

KNIG

9 10 52

ROYAL COLLEGE OF ART

KENSINGTON GORE

Prince's Gate

Synagogue

Rutland Gate

Rutland Gardens

Trevor St.

Raphael St.

Tattersha Taver

KENSINGTON ROAD

3

9 10 52

ROYAL ALBERT HALL

ROYAL GEOGRAPHICAL SOCIETY

PRINCE'S GATE GARDENS

Ennismore

Russian Orthodox Cathedral

Trevor Place

TREVOR SQUARE

PO

35

Bremner Rd.

Prince Albert

Albert Court

COLLEGE SPORTS COMPLEX

MONTPELIER SQUARE

KNIGHTSB. STATIO

Holy Trinity

Prince Consort Road

ROYAL COLLEGE OF MUSIC

MUSEUM OF MUSICAL INSTRUMENTS

EXHIBITION

PRINCE'S GARDENS

Ennismore Gardens

ENNISMORE GARDENS

Ennismore Gardens

Ennismore

Rutland Gate

Montpelier Street

St.

Montpelier Walk

Montpelier Place

American Express

ROAD

Han

4

IMPERIAL COLLEGE

ALBERTOPOLIS

Gdns. Mews

Ava Gardner's Monument

34

Ennismore Street

Ennismore Gardens Mews

Cheval Place

BROMPTON SQUARE

Crown & Sceptre

EMPORIO ARMANI

C1 C4 74 414

Brompton Place

HARRODS

Hans Roa

QUEEN'S TOWER (300ft.)

SCIENCE MUSEUM

PO

VICTORIA & ALBERT MUSEUM

GAMBLE ROOM

Holy Trinity

AUSTIN REED

Bunch of Grapes

Ovington Gdns.

Beauchamp Pl.

BEAUFORT GARDENS

Walton Place

St Savi

HENRY COLE WING

Fountain

BROMPTON ORATORY

Yeoman's Row

OVINGTON SQUARE

St. Columba's

Por

5

70 360

NATURAL HISTORY MUSEUM

ROAD

Memorial Place

THURLOE PLACE

CROMWELL GDNS.

P

REMBRANDT

BROMPTON

EGERTON GARDENS

Egerton Gdns.

Egerton Ter.

Egerton Crescent

The Enterprise

PS

LENNOX GARDENS

LENNOX GARDENS MEWS

74

CROMWELL ROAD

Cromwell

Thurloe

THURLOE SQUARE

Alexander Pl.

South Terrace

Walton Street

Hasker St.

Ovington St.

First St.

The Australian

SORBONNE

LYCÉE FRANÇAIS

Queensbury Place

INSTITUT FRANÇAIS

MOAT HOUSE

74

Thurloe St.

70 345

SOUTH KENSINGTON

The Hour Glass

Ives Street

Mossop St.

Denyer St.

Milner St.

Halsey St.

Moo

QUEEN'S GATE

70 74 360

Harrington

Bute St.

Road

49

BROMPTON

Road

Pelham

360

Street

Draycott

Admiral Codrington

Rawlings St.

Rosemoor Street

Cadog

6

49

St. Augustine

PO

Thomas Cook

Onslow Square

Pelham Place

C1 49 345 414

THE CONRAN SHOP

SLOANE

360

AVENUE

Avenue

PS

JURYS KENSINGTON

REGENCY

Old Brompton

C1

Summer Pl.

ONSLOW SQUARE

Pelham Cres.

Sydney Place

FULHAM ROAD

Elystan Place

Lucan worth

Lecworth Place

A

B

14 49 345 414

▼ 44

C

360

D

ADORNED WITH A FIG LEAF THE 18-FOOT-HIGH STATUE OF ACHILLES WAS CAST FROM CANNONS CAPTURED BY THE DUKE OF WELLINGTON: IT WAS A TRIBUTE TO THE DUKE FUNDED FROM SUBSCRIPTION BY 'LADIES OF QUALITY'

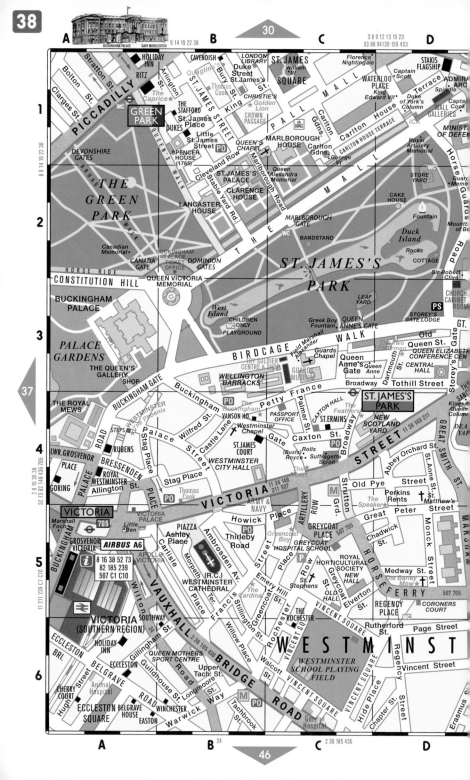

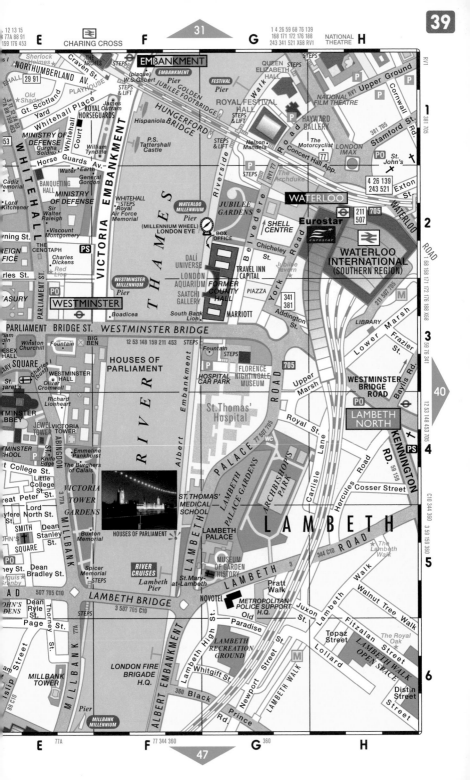

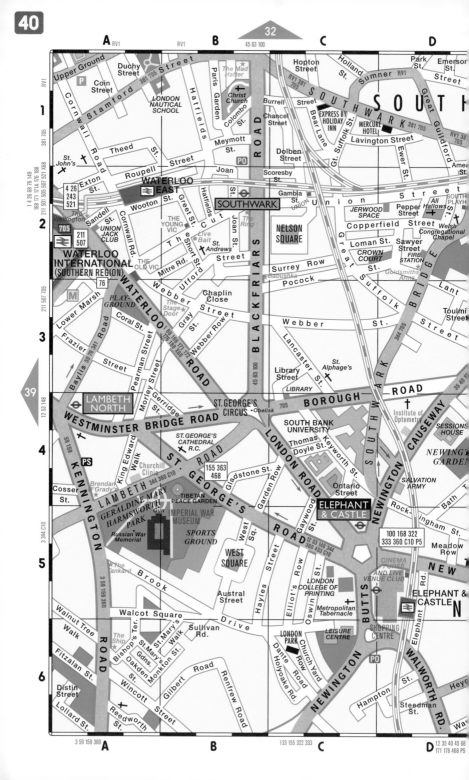

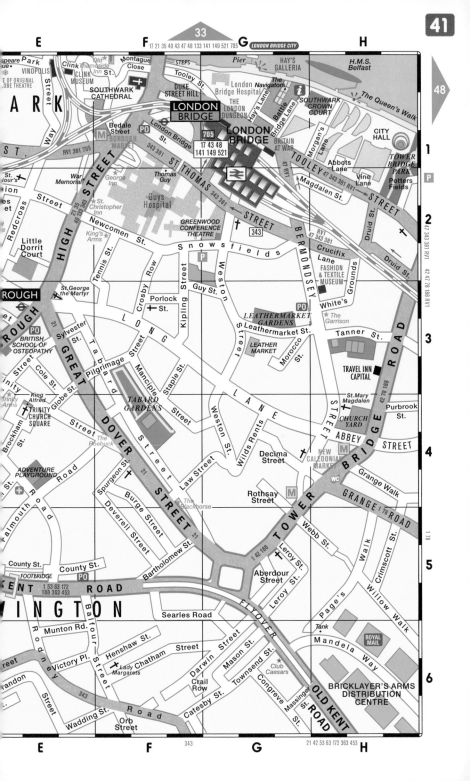

48

E F 33 G LONDON BRIDGE CITY H

17 21 35 40 43 47 48 133 141 149 521 705

Shakespeare Park
VINOPOLIS
HE OF ORIGINAL GLOBE THEATRE

Clink St.
Old Thameside Inn
CLINK MUSEUM

SOUTHWARK CATHEDRAL

Bedale Street
BOROUGH MARKET

Montague Close

STEPS
Tooley St.
DUKE STREET HILL
London Bridge Hospital

Pier
London Bridge

THE LONDON DUNGEON

HAY'S GALLERIA

The Navigators

H.M.S. Belfast

LONDON BRIDGE

705

London Bridge

LONDON BRIDGE

17 43 48
141 149 521

BRITAIN AT WAR

SOUTHWARK CROWN COURT

The Queen's Walk

CITY HALL

TOWER BRIDGE PARK

P

Potters Fields

RV1 381 705

St. our's

ion es

HIGH STREET

PO

303 381

ST. THOMAS

343 381

STREET

Thomas Guy

Magdalen St.

Abbots Lane

Vine Lane

TOOLEY 47 47 381 RV1

BERMONDSEY

42 478 188 RV1

1

42 343 381 RV1

Redcross

Street

Little Dorrit Court

War Memorial
George Inn
St. Christopher Inn

King's Arms

Guys Hospital

Newcomen St.

Tennis St.

GREENWOOD CONFERENCE THEATRE

343

Snowsfields

Weston Street

Guy St.

Crucifix Lane

FASHION & TEXTILE MUSEUM

White's

The Garrison

Tanner St.

Druid St.

DRUID STREET

2

ROUGH

St. George the Martyr

PO

BRITISH SCHOOL OF OSTEOPATHY

Sylvester St.

Cole St.

Globe St.

GREAT DOVER

Tabard St.

Crosby Row

Porlock St.

Kipling Street

Staple St.

LEATHERMARKET GARDENS

Leathermarket St.

LEATHER MARKET

PO

Morocco St.

St. Mary Magdalen

CHURCH YARD

TRAVEL INN CAPITAL

ABBEY STREET

Purbrook St.

TOWER BRIDGE ROAD

3

Trinity Arms

King Alfred

TRINITY CHURCH SQUARE

Brockham St.

DOVER

Pilgrimage Street

TABARD GARDENS

The Roebuck

Manciple Street

Weston St.

Wilds Rents

Decima Street

NEW CALEDONIAN MARKET

M

WC

GRANGE

4

ADVENTURE PLAYGROUND

Falmouth Road

STREET

Spurgeon St.

Burge Street

Deverell Street

Law Street

The Blackhorse

Rothsay Street

M

Grange Walk

GRANGE ROAD

1 78

Crimscott St.

Willow Walk

5

County St.

FOOTBRIDGE

PO

Bartholomew Street

Aberdour Street

Leroy St.

Webb St.

Page's Walk

1 53 63 172
188 363 453

KENT ROAD

Searles Road

FLYOVER

Leroy

Mandela Way

ROYAL MAIL

WINGTON

Rodney Street

Munton Rd.

Victory Pl.

Henshaw St.

Lady Margarets

Street

Balfour Street

Darwin Street

Mason St.

Townsend St.

Congreve St.

Club Caesars

Tank

OLD KENT ROAD

BRICKLAYER'S ARMS DISTRIBUTION CENTRE

6

brandon

343

Road

Wadding St.

Orb Street

Crail Row

Catesby St.

Massinger St.

E F 343 G 21 42 53 63 172 363 453 H

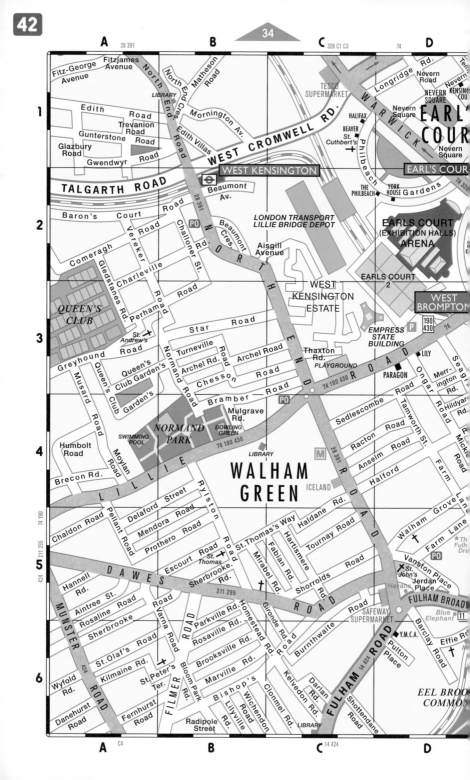

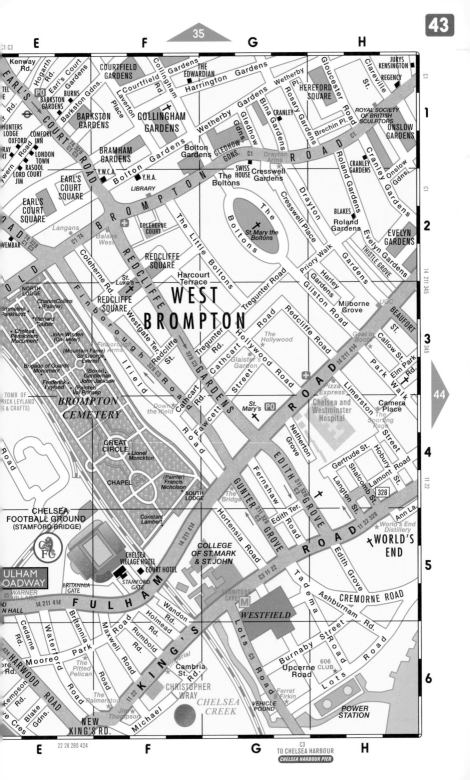

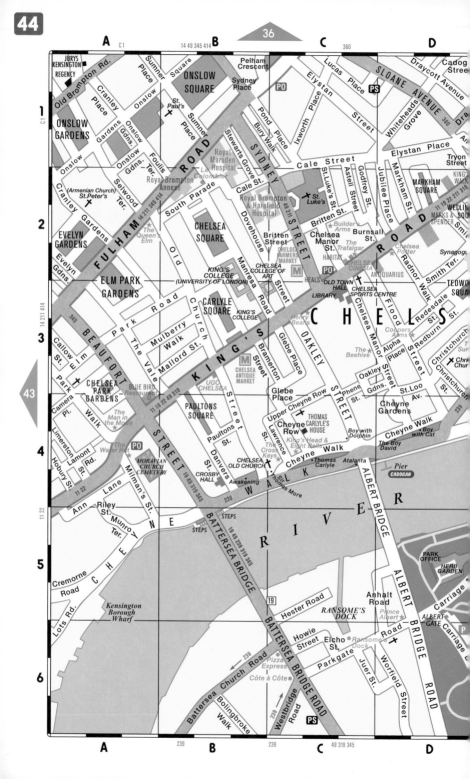

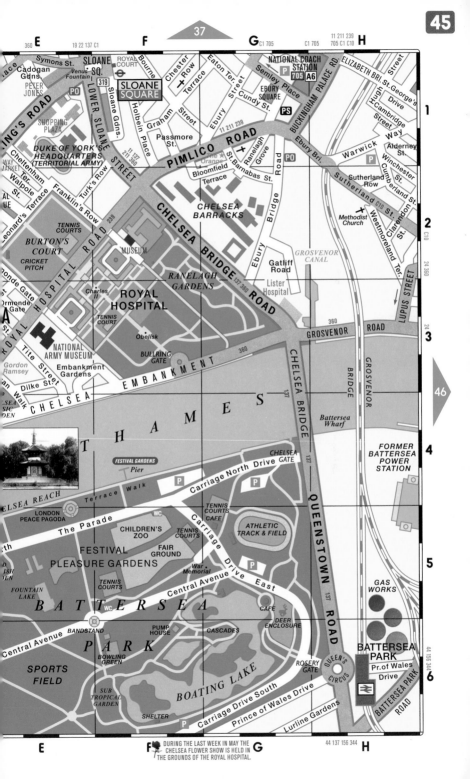

E 360 19 22 137 C1 **F** 37 **G** C1 705 C1 705 11 211 239 705 C1 C10 **H**

Cadogan Gdns **SLOANE SQ.** ROYAL COURT Bourne Chester Row Eaton Ter. Semley Place NATIONAL COACH STATION 705 A6 Elizabeth Bri. St. St.George's Street

Peter Jones Symons St. Venus Fountain Holbein Place Terrace Graham Street Cundy St. EBURY SQUARE PS Buckingham Palace Rd. Hugh Street Cambridge Street Drive

PO **SLOANE SQUARE** 319 Sloane Gdns. Ebury Street Ebury 11 211 239 211 380 Ebury Bri. PO Warwick Way Alderney St.

SHOPPING PLAZA KING'S ROAD LOWER SLOANE STREET Passmore St. **PIMLICO ROAD** St. Barnabas St. Ranelagh Grove Ebury Bridge Road Sutherland Row Winchester St. Cumberland St.

DUKE OF YORK'S HEADQUARTERS (TERRITORIAL ARMY) Cheltenham Ter. Walpole Terrace Franklin's Row Turk's Row Bloomfield Terrace Orange St. **CHELSEA BARRACKS** Ebury Bridge Methodist Church Sutherland Row Clarendon Westmoreland Ter. C10 C10

TENNIS COURTS BURTON'S COURT CRICKET PITCH HOSPITAL ROAD 239 MUSEUM **CHELSEA BRIDGE ROAD** Ebury Bridge Gatliff Road GROSVENOR CANAL Lister Hospital LUPUS STREET 24 360 C10

A Ormonde Gate Leonard's Gate TENNIS COURT Charles II **ROYAL HOSPITAL** RANELAGH GARDENS 360 GROSVENOR ROAD 360 24

Tite Street Gordon Ramsey NATIONAL ARMY MUSEUM Obelisk Embankment Gardens BULLRING GATE 360 **CHELSEA EMBANKMENT** CHELSEA BRIDGE GROSVENOR BRIDGE 46

Dilke Street **T H A M E S** Battersea Wharf FORMER BATTERSEA POWER STATION 4

CHELSEA REACH FESTIVAL GARDENS Pier Terrace Walk P CHELSEA GATE Carriage North Drive 137

LONDON PEACE PAGODA The Parade WC CHILDREN'S ZOO Carriage Drive TENNIS COURTS CAFE ATHLETIC TRACK & FIELD P QUEENSTOWN ROAD GAS WORKS 5

FESTIVAL PLEASURE GARDENS FAIR GROUND TENNIS COURTS War Memorial P 137

FOUNTAIN LAKE TENNIS COURTS Central Avenue WC CAFE DEER ENCLOSURE BATTERSEA PARK Pr.of Wales Drive 44 156 344 6

B A T T E R S E A P A R K BANDSTAND PUMP HOUSE CASCADES CAFE Queen's Rosery Gate QUEEN'S CIRCUS BATTERSEA PARK ROAD

Central Avenue SPORTS FIELD BOWLING GREEN SUB TROPICAL GARDEN **BOATING LAKE** SHELTER P Carriage Drive South Prince of Wales Drive Lurline Gardens

E **F** 44 137 156 344 **G** **H**

DURING THE LAST WEEK IN MAY THE CHELSEA FLOWER SHOW IS HELD IN THE GROUNDS OF THE ROYAL HOSPITAL.

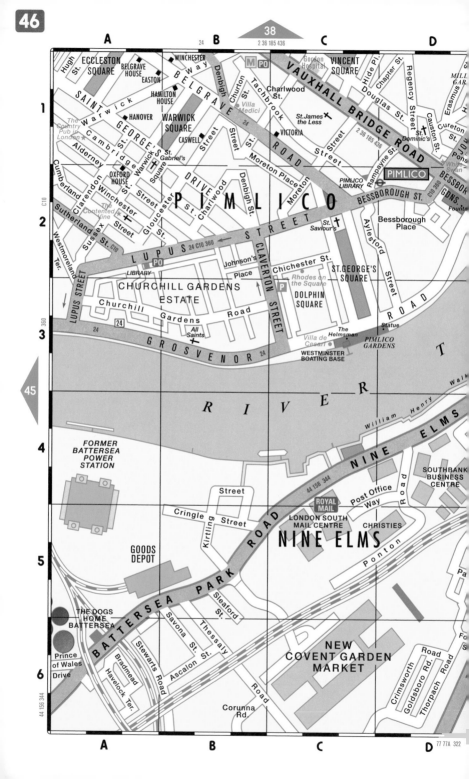

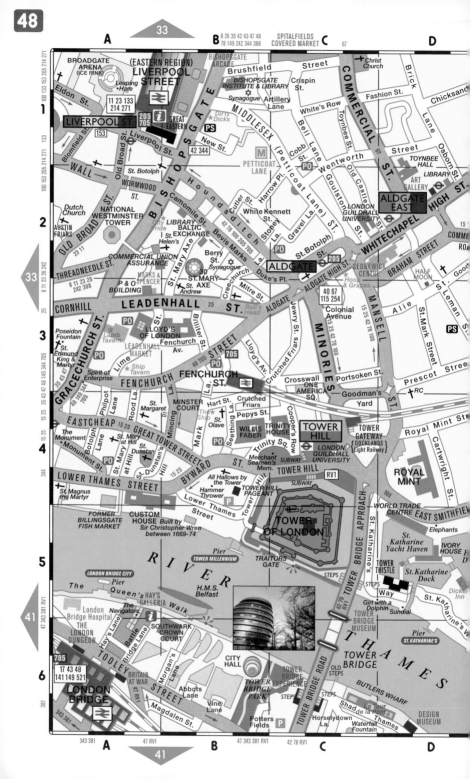

THE TOWER OF LONDON

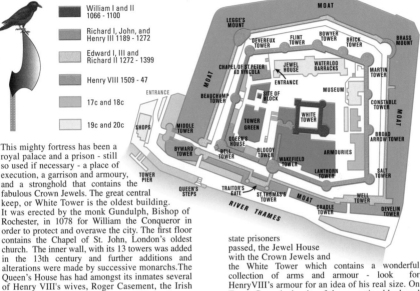

William I and II
1066 - 1100

Richard I, John, and
Henry III 1189 - 1272

Edward I, III and
Richard II 1272 - 1399

Henry VIII 1509 - 47

17c and 18c

19c and 20c

This mighty fortress has been a royal palace and a prison - still so used if necessary - a place of execution, a garrison and armoury, and a stronghold that contains the fabulous Crown Jewels. The great central keep, or White Tower is the oldest building. It was erected by the monk Gundulph, Bishop of Rochester, in 1078 for William the Conqueror in order to protect and overawe the city. The first floor contains the Chapel of St. John, London's oldest church. The inner wall, with its 13 towers was added in the 13th century and further additions and alterations were made by successive monarchs. The Queen's House has had amongst its inmates several of Henry VIII's wives, Roger Casement, the Irish revolutionary and Rudolf Hess, Hitler's deputy. Other notable features to interest the visitor include the Bloody Tower, with its portcullis, where Sir Walter Raleigh began to write his unfinished "History of the World", Traitors' Gate through which

state prisoners passed, the Jewel House with the Crown Jewels and the White Tower which contains a wonderful collection of arms and armour - look for Henry VIII's armour for an idea of his real size. On Tower Green is the site of the execution block and the tower ravens. Always here are the Yeoman Warders - Beefeaters - in their traditional uniform.
Daily March - Oct 9.00 - 17.00, Suns 10.00 - 17.00.
Nov - Feb 9.00 - 16.00, Suns & Mons 10.00. Charge

RIVER AND CANAL TRIPS

RIVER TRIPS Splendid trips are available on the River Thames during the summer months. In the evenings there are also supper trips for that special family or romantic occasion. These regular boat services run the whole length of the river, from April to October, when they revert to winter schedules. Within the London area there are daily services from Westminster Bridge, upriver to Kew Gardens, Hampton Court, and the riverside at Richmond, and downriver to the Tower of London, Greenwich and the Thames Barrier. Supper cruises also embark from Westminster Pier.
From Charing Cross Pier there are services to and from Tower Bridge and Greenwich.
From the rail terminals at Waterloo and Paddington there are combined Rail-River trips going to and from Windsor, Staines, Maidenhead, Marlow, Oxford and other attractive places along the river.
Full information on these trips is available from
Charing Cross Pier (map ref. F6 31)　☎ *7987 1185*
Westminster Pier (F3 39)　　　　　　☎ *7930 9033*
London Tourist Board　　　　　☎ *0839 123432*

THE THAMES BARRIER This remarkable piece of engineering is the world's largest moveable defense against flooding. Cruises from the flood barrier embark from Westminster Pier and Lambeth Pier stopping at Canary Wharf and Greenwich.　　　　　☎ *7930 3373*

CANAL TRIPS Frequent waterbus services run on the Regent's Canal by the London Waterbus Company starting from Little Venice, Paddington (G1 27), passing through Regent's Park to the London Zoo.
Inclusive Waterbus and Zoo tickets can be bought.
There are also narrow boat cruises from Blomfield Road (Little Venice) to Camden Lock and from Camden Lock to the Zoo and Little Venice.
London Waterbus Company
Camden Lock, NW1　　　　　☎ *7482 2550*
Jason's Trip runs from Little Venice to Camden Lock in an original painted narrow boat along the Grand Union Canal and the Regent's Canal.
Restaurant. Snacks, beer, wine, soft drinks on sale.
Booking Office　　　　　☎ *7286 3428*
There are "Jenny Wren" cruises on the Regent's Canal in traditionally decorated narrow boats through the Zoo, Regent's Park and Maida Hill tunnel.
250 Camden High Street, NW1　　☎ *7485 4433*
The "Fair Lady" narrow boat has a restaurant and runs dinner cruises from Tuesday to Saturday 19.30 or 20.00 hours, and lunch cruises on Sundays 12.30 or 13.00 hours but booking in advance for these is essential at Camden Lock Office.
277 Camden High Street, NW1　　☎ *7485 6210*

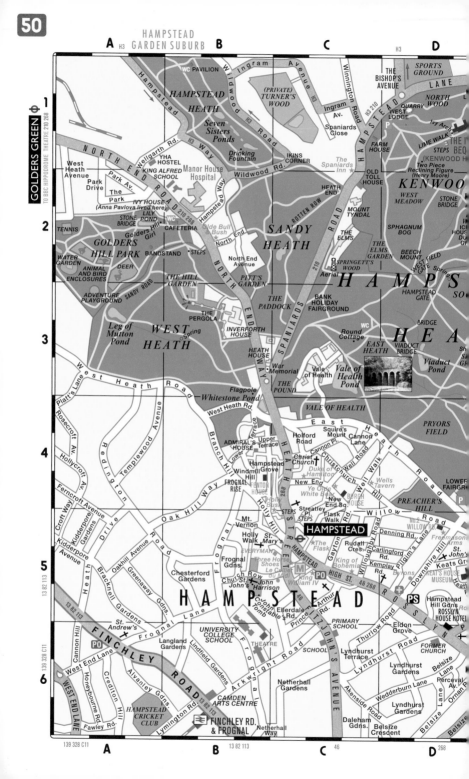

HAMPSTEAD
GARDEN SUBURB

A H3   **B**   **C**   H3   **D**

PAVILION
WC

Ingram   Avenue H3

Winnington Road

THE
BISHOP'S
AVENUE

SPORTS
GROUND

LANE

1

HAMPSTEAD
HEATH

(PRIVATE)
TURNER'S
WOOD

Ingram
Av.

Spaniards
Close

H3 210

QUARRY

NORTH
WOOD

WEST
LODGE

Ivy Arch

Wildwood Road

Seven
Sisters
Ponds

HAMPSTEAD ROAD

P

LIME WALK
STEPS

THE IV
BE

Hampstead Road

H3 Way

Drinking
Fountain

IKINS
CORNER

FARM
HOUSE

The
Spaniards
Inn ★

OLD
TOLL
HOUSE

Two Piece
Reclining Figure
(Henry Moore)

KENWOO

YHA
HOSTEL

KING ALFRED
SCHOOL

Manor House
Hospital

Wildwood Rd.

HEATH
END

MOUNT
TYNDAL

WEST
MEADOW

STONE
BRIDGE

West
Heath
Avenue

Wellgarth Rd.

ROTTEN ROW

210

NORTH END ROAD 210 268

Park Av.

Hampstead Way

SANDY
HEATH

THE
ELMS

SPHAGNUM
BOG

ICE
HOUS
DU

West
Park
Drive

The
Park

IVY HOUSE
(Anna Pavlova lived here)

LILY
POND

STONE
BRIDGE

WC

Olde Bull
& Bush

THE
ELMS
GARDEN

BEECH
MOUNT

WEST FIELD
GATE   Spring

2

TENNIS

GOLDERS
HILL PARK

Golders Hill
Girl

CAFETERIA

North End

North End
Avenue

SPRINGETT'S
WOOD

HAMPSTEAD
GATE

SO

WATER
GARDEN

BANDSTAND

STEPS

SPANIARDS

Aerial

HAMPS

ANIMAL
AND BIRD
ENCLOSURES

DEER

Sandy Road

THE HILL
GARDEN

PITT'S
GARDEN

THE
PADDOCK

BANK
HOLIDAY
FAIRGROUND

HE A

ADVENTURE
PLAYGROUND

NORTH END WAY

THE
PERGOLA

INVERFORTH
HOUSE

WC

BRIDGE

3

WEST
HEATH

Spring

HEATH
HOUSE

THE
POUND

Round
Cottage

EAST
HEATH

Vale of
Health

Vale of Health
Pond

VIADUCT
BRIDGE

Viaduct
Pond

Sh
GR

Leg of
Mutton
Pond

War
Memorial

Vale
of Health

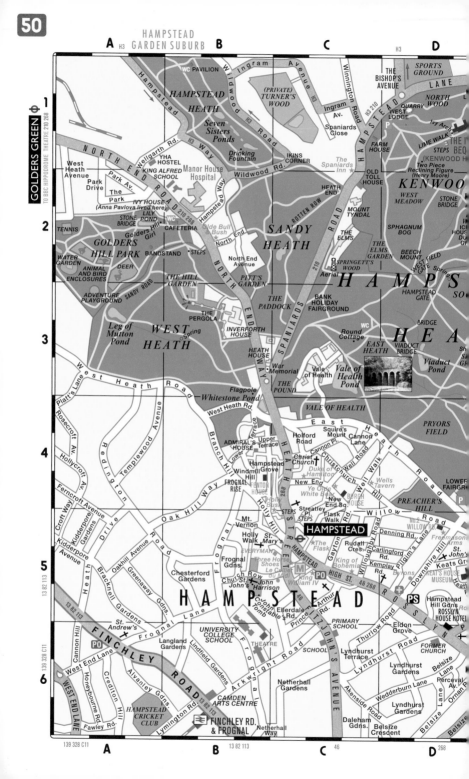

West Heath Road

Flagpole
Whitestone Pond

West Heath Rd.

VALE OF HEALTH

PRYORS
FIELD

Platt's Lane

SPANIARDS ROAD

East

Squire's
Mount

Cannon
Lane

Rosecroft Av.

West Heath Road

Redington Road

Templewood Avenue

Branch Hill

HEATH STREET

ADMIRAL'S
HOUSE

Upper
Terrace

Lower
Terrace

Holford
Road

Christ
Church ✝

Cannon Pl.

Christchurch Hill

Well Walk

Wells
Tavern

Well Road

LOWER
FAIRGR

4

Hollycroft Av.

Oak Hill Way

Frognal Rise

Hampstead
Grove

Windmill
Hill

FENTON
HOUSE

New End

Duke of
Hamilton

Ye Olde
White Bear

New
End Sq.

BURGH
HOUSE

P

PREACHER'S
HILL

Ferncroft Avenue

Mt.
Vernon

Holly
Walk

St.
Mary's

Streatley
Pl.

Flask
Walk

Willow

Road

WILLOW RD.

No.2

Croft Way

Kidderpore
Gardens

Kidderpore
Avenue

Heath Drive

Oakhill Avenue

Greenaway Gdns.

Frognal

Chesterford
Gardens

Holly
Walk

Church Row

St.
John's

Three Horse
Shoes

Le Cellier
du Midi

STEPS

HAMPSTEAD

The
Flask

Denning Rd.

Rudall
Cres.

Carlingford
Rd.

Gayton Rd.

Kemplay Rd.

King of
Bohemia

Freemasons
Arms

St.
John's

Downshire Hill

Keats Grove

KEATS HOUSE
MUSEUM

5

Bracknell Gardens

Frognal Gdns.

ch Row

HAMPSTEAD HIGH ST.

M

PO

William IV

46 268

Byrons

ROSSLYN

PS

Hampstead
Hill Gdns

ROSSLYN
HOUSE HOTEL

H A M P S T E A D

St.
Andrew's

Frognal Lane

Lindfield Gardens

John
Harrison

John
Constable's
Tomb

Ellerdale Rd.

Prince Arthur Rd.

FITZJOHN'S AVENUE

PRIMARY
SCHOOL

Thurlow Road

Eldon
Grove

FORMER
CHURCH

Cannon Hill

West End Lane

PO

Alvanley Gdns.

Crediton Hill

UNIVERSITY
COLLEGE
SCHOOL

Langland
Gardens

Arkwright Road

THEATRE

SCHOOL

Lyndhurst
Terrace

Lyndhurst
Gardens

Belsize
Lane

Perceval Av.

6

Honeybourne Rd.

Fawley Rd.

FINCHLEY ROAD

13 82 113

HAMPSTEAD
CRICKET
CLUB

Lymington Rd.

CAMDEN
ARTS CENTRE

🚆 FINCHLEY RD.
& FROGNAL

Netherhall
Gardens

Netherhall
Way

Akenside Road

Wedderburn Lane

Lyndhurst
Gardens

Daleham
Gdns.

Belsize
Crescent

Belsize

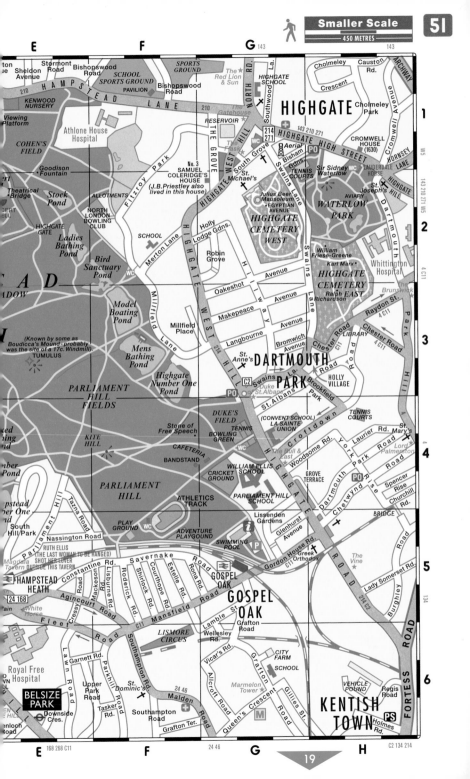

THE LONDON ZOO

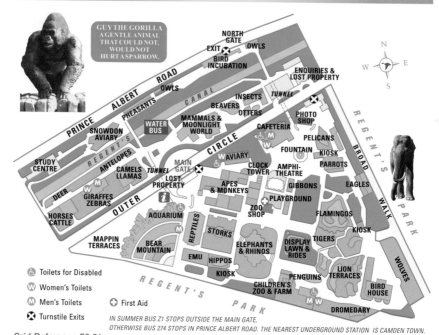

GUY THE GORILLA
A GENTLE ANIMAL
THAT COULD NOT,
WOULD NOT
HURT A SPARROW.

NORTH GATE
EXIT
OWLS
BIRD INCUBATION
ENQUIRIES & LOST PROPERTY
ROAD
ALBERT
OWLS
CANAL
INSECTS
TUNNEL
PHEASANTS
BEAVERS
OTTERS
PHOTO SHOP
PRINCE
SNOWDON AVIARY
WATER BUS
MAMMALS & MOONLIGHT WORLD
CAFETERIA
REGENT'S
ANTELOPES
CIRCLE
PELICANS
REGENT'S PARK
STUDY CENTRE
CAMELS LLAMAS
TUNNEL
MAIN GATE
AVIARY
FOUNTAIN
KIOSK
LOST PROPERTY
CLOCK TOWER
AMPHI-THEATRE
PARROTS
DEER
GIRAFFES ZEBRAS
OUTER
APES & MONKEYS
GIBBONS
EAGLES
HORSES CATTLE
AQUARIUM
ZOO SHOP
PLAYGROUND
FLAMINGOS
BROAD WALK
MAPPIN TERRACES
REPTILES
STORKS
DISPLAY LAWN & RIDES
TIGERS
KIOSK
BEAR MOUNTAIN
ELEPHANTS & RHINOS
EMU
HIPPOS
LION TERRACES
WOLVES
REGENT'S
KIOSK
PENGUINS
BIRD HOUSE
CHILDREN'S ZOO & FARM
PARK
DROMEDARY

Toilets for Disabled
Women's Toilets
Men's Toilets
First Aid
Turnstile Exits

IN SUMMER BUS Z1 STOPS OUTSIDE THE MAIN GATE,
OTHERWISE BUS 274 STOPS IN PRINCE ALBERT ROAD. THE NEAREST UNDERGROUND STATION IS CAMDEN TOWN.

Grid Reference F2 21

The London Zoo is one of the oldest and most famous animal collections in the world and, together with Whipsnade Park in Bedfordshire, forms part of the Zoological Society of London, a scientific society founded by Sir Stamford Raffles and others in 1826. The zoo extends over an area of 36 acres in Regent's Park. More than 12,000 animals live here, including lions, giraffes, elephants, and many other species of mammals together with birds, reptiles, amphibians, fishes and insects. A high proportion of the animals were born here but many others come from other zoos throughout the world.

I loved this zoo as a child and still do try to visit London and Whipsnade twice a year. My father always had a particular fascination for the gentle gorillas and *Guy* in particular, who always gave you that quizzical look, weighing you up as much as you were him. Alas he is long gone, as is my father, but *Guy's* statue stands in the zoo and always jogs my memory of happy bygone days.

There is a pavilion for Apes and Monkeys, where the gorillas, orang-utans, chimpanzees, gibbons and monkeys are to be found; while in another Pavilion for Small Mammals there are primates, rodents, carnivores and aquatic mammals. The largest mammals, the elephants and rhinoceroses, dwell in fine modern quarters designed by Sir Hugh Casson in 1965: on the Mappin Terraces you will find the sloth bears. (It appears to be too cruel to put the polar bears in this environment). Underneath the terraces is the Aquarium which stretches for 150 yards, (Britains largest), with fishes from fresh, sea, and tropical waters all over the world. Seawater in the circulation system is topped up annually when it is brought in by road-tanker from the North Sea. Here you find deadly piranha fish with razor-sharp teeth,

gently drifting seahorses, poisonous dragon fish, eels, lobsters and crabs. In the nearby Reptile House, all the major groups of reptiles are represented - turtles and terrapins, tortoises, crocodiles and alligators, brilliant coloured and camouflaged lizards, and snakes from the venomous to the benign, with vipers, pythons and boa constrictors.

Animal feeding times are staggered throughout the day and many visitors like to plan their passage through the zoo taking account of these times. Check the timetable when you enter the zoo.

The penguins always look important and are a favourite to watch. They have a superb pool with spiral interlocking ramps designed way back in the 1930's by Berthold Lubetkin. I like the way they move along in a queue-like procession, as though they are waiting for the bus back to Antarctica.

The Lion Terraces are a marvellous improvement on the old barred cages, for the cats now live in open areas, rich with plants and grasses that reflect their natural habitat. Inside the Bird House are many beautiful species, including brilliant coloured parrots, big beaked toucans and hornbills. The largest birds in the world are to be found in the Stork and Ostrich House. Surely guaranteed to make you shudder, the Insect House contains great colonies of ants, praying mantises, stick insects, spiders and scorpions.

A particularly fascinating collection of creatures is assembled in the Moonlight World where assimilated 'night' is created to encourage nocturnal animals to become active in normal daytime. There are badgers, bush babies, flying foxes, lorises and douroucouli, the only nocturnal monkey in the world.

Open daily except Christmas Day.
Summer 10.00 - 17.30 April - September.
Winter 10.00 - 16.00. *Charge*

LONDON'S PARKS AND VILLAGES

London is made especially beautiful by the wealth of its green open spaces, and its majestic squares that break the monotony of the grey buildings with their lovely flower-filled gardens. The largest and principal London parks are the Royal Parks, which are Crown property and are open to the public free.

The Royal Parks

THE GREEN PARK Located between Piccadilly and Constitution Hill, this is a relaxing park that is full of mature trees and grassland.
HYDE PARK With the adjoining Kensington Gardens, the park extends to 600 acres of grassland, trees and flower beds, with the Serpentine Lake for boating and fishing (only with a permit), and at the Lido, bathing. restaurants, band concerts, horse riding in Rotten Row, football, bowling and putting.
KENSINGTON GARDENS A former hunting ground laid out by William III, adjoining the west side of Hyde Park and creating a complete contrast - it is a more pleasant and peaceful place. There are Italian Gardens, the Round Pond for model boating, Long Water, the Peter Pan statue and the Albert Memorial.
PRIMROSE HILL From the summit of this grassy hill which is 68 metres (206ft) above sea level, there is a superb panorama of London. An engraved plaque identifies the buildings for you.
REGENT'S PARK A truly lovely park, framed by the beautiful terraced architecture of John Nash who designed this park at the request of the Prince Regent (later George IV). A rose garden, magnificent shrubs and trees, lawns, fountains, rowing on the lake, band concerts, the magical Open-Air Theatre and the Zoo are all part of this great park.
ST. JAMES'S PARK A one time deer park and now very beautiful with a picturesque bridge over an ornamental lake. Many wildfowl, pelicans and geese, fine views and band concerts.

Public Parks and Spaces

BATTERSEA PARK On the southside of the Thames, and the scene of the annual Easter parade. The Peace Pagoda (E5 45) was built in 1985 by Japanese monks to commemorate the tragic bombing of Hiroshima.
HAMPSTEAD HEATH They call the heath 'the lungs of London' and so it is. The heath is 792 acres of pure joy, great for flying kites, for walks through dells and uplands, for woods and unusual fauna. There are lakes for model boats, and swimming and fishing; animal enclosures and ornamental gardens: the Hill Garden (B3 50) with its pergola is well worth seeking out. On summer evenings Kenwood is a lovely setting for the open air Lakeside concerts from opera companies and symphony orchestras.
I always enjoy a brisk walk over the heath with my wife after the excesses of Christmas.
HOLLAND PARK In the heart of Kensington and for the early part of the 20th century, a private garden. Includes a Japanese garden and an open air theatre.
WATERLOW PARK A favourite park of mine situated on top of Highgate Hill. Undulating, small and interesting at every turn, with recreational features, an aviary and Lauderdale House for musical events - classical and jazz.

> **THE ROOF GARDENS** In Kensington near Derry Street (E3 27) on the very top of a building that used to be occupied by Derry & Toms there is an absolutely magnificent and unique rooftop paradise garden; for two days (Thurs. & Sats.) a club and restaurant. Owned by Richard Branson, you can view this when there are no functions.

London's Villages

Before the 19th century and the expansion of the railways London was contained within the City, Westminster and Southwark. The communities that were outside these areas were villages. As transport extended, the villages became a part of the conurbation. Here are a few of the villages that are still discernible within the great conurbation.
HAMPSTEAD Page 50-51. When you arrive at Hampstead on the underground you are 64 metres below ground level in the deepest station in London, and on reaching the surface you know you are in a different atmosphere. For many years, Hampstead has been a haven for arts of all descriptions. John Constable who did many paintings of the heath is buried in the churchyard of St.John's (B5 50), as is John Harrison, the self-taught clockmaker who is attributed with defining 'Longitude' by means of his chronometer. The flagpole (B3 50) at the top of Heath Street is the highest point in London, although the best view is from the top of Parliament Hill. Legends of the highwayman, Dick Turpin, are rife in old pubs like *The Spaniards*, while many of the little back streets reveal surprising architecture mixed in with the cottages. There are numerous cafes and bistros and the fresh air on the heath is therapeutic.
Kenwood House On the north side of the heath is this 17th century Robert Adam house, which has a fine collection of paintings, a Rembrandt self-portrait and works by Turner, Romney, Vermeer, Hals etc. The superb Adam Library is a feature worth looking out for. *Daily April - Sept 10.00 - 18.00 October - March 10.00 - 16.00* *Free*
HIGHGATE Page 51. Highgate has even more of a village atmosphere. Perched on the top of a hill, it deceptively seems higher than its neighbour Hampstead. I have already mentioned Waterlow Park which is extremely pleasant, particularly during the week. The famous pub is *The Flask* (G1 51), which dates back to 1767. On summer evenings the tables are filled with people enjoying the ale and food. John Betjeman loved the pub and they say Major Rogers, the frontiersman of 'Rogers Rangers' fame drank here - do you remember Spencer Tracy in the film *Northwest Passage*? Strangely, the biggest attraction in Highgate is the cemetery, for here Karl Marx was put to rest - his memorial is very striking and strong as though it was made forever. In the village there are many international restaurants, and further down Highgate Hill there is a friendly Brazilian restaurant, *Sabor do Brasil,* that features a bossa-nova group on Wednesday evenings.
ISLINGTON Page 24. Home of many intellectuals and artists, not as ostentatious as Chelsea and always full of life. It has an antique shop mall and an antiques market; some great and famous fringe pub theatres like the *King's Head* (B1 24), where often a future West End or Broadway production can be seen in embryo form; incidently the pub still rings your bar bill up in old shillings and pence! Islington is always enjoyable: there are many bookshops, cafes and restaurants serving every cuisine imaginable: *Le Mercure* and *Art to Zen* in Upper Street both serve excellent food and will not break your pocket; for more formal dining, *Frederick's* may suit you more. The Victorian pub, the *Camden Head*, has great atmosphere and good lunches (C1 16), and is also a comedy venue.

ENTERTAINMENTS

London is world renowned for excellent and varied entertainments, especially music and theatre. For details the Saturday *Guardian* newspaper has a free supplement.There are also many free listing papers that you might find in your hotel lobby. *Time Out* publish a listing magazine, and there is always the *Big Issue* which helps the homeless.

Concert Halls

BARBICAN HALL   **E1 33**
Silk Street, EC2.   ☎ *7638 8891*
This is the spiritual home of the London Symphony Orchestra. The hall also plays host to some of the leading orchestras in the world. Seating over 2000, with good sight lines and acoustics that have been improved over the years.

ROYAL ALBERT HALL   **A3 36**
Kensington Gore, SW7.   ☎ *7589 8212*
Built in 1871 as a memorial to the Prince Consort,

this huge, beautiful amphitheatre with a dome of iron and glass can hold over 8000 within its circumference. The hall is not only used for classical music; there are all kinds of entertainment and sports held here. But it is the summertime Promenade Concerts which endears it to Londoners. The programmes of the *Proms* are always diverse and interesting (compared with the average concert). The last night is a memorable festive occasion. The organ is tremendous - I once remember nearly falling off my seat when the organ entered at the start of the Poulenc organ concerto!

ROYAL FESTIVAL HALL   **A3 36**
South Bank, SE1.   ☎ *7960 4242*
Described by Aram Khachaturian as a large wheat granary when it was built for the Festival of Britain way back in 1951, this 2600 seat hall with its elm panels and excellent acoustics is still going strong. Intervals at the Festival Hall are always good; as long as you order your drinks before going in, you can leisurely walk around and view the river from the terrace. Even better is a meal before the concert - the restaurant is spacious and you may even have one of the artists sitting near you. There is a good bookshop and CD shop.
Queen Elizabeth Hall Situated close by, with less than half the capacity of the Festival Hall, this is a more intimate venue suited for small orchestras or jazz orientated music.
Purcell Room Even smaller still; this is an ideal place to hear a piano recital or small jazz combo. The Queen Elizabeth and the Purcell Room are both comfortable venues, but the exteriors are very stark indeed which is unfortunate.

WIGMORE HALL   **H3 29**
Wigmore Street, W1.   ☎ *7935 2141*
An elegant hall with plenty of marble and alabaster, forever linked with the piano manufacturer Bechstein who had the hall built to showcase his pianos (his shop was next door). It is a comfortable place for classical and jazz music, with very good acoustics.

ST. JOHN'S, SMITH SQUARE   **E5 39**
Smith Square, SW1.   ☎ *7222 1061*
Used by the BBC for its lunchtime chamber concerts, this Baroque building is a popular venue for the office workers in the Westminster area.

Opera and Ballet

As a small boy my mother deposited me outside Sadlers Wells into the care of a school teacher friend for my initiation into Opera. I did not want to go and never said I enjoyed the experience. I did though, and I have loved Opera ever since. Opera today is very expensive and unfortunately a good seat for Covent Garden makes it a very special occasion. The English National Opera and Sadlers Wells are less expensive and they do have some very adventurous productions in very good theatres.

LONDON COLISEUM   **E5 31**
St.Martin's Lane, WC2.   ☎ *7632 8300*
The flashing globe makes this 1904 Romansque style theatre instantly recognisable. Built by Oswald Stoll, it is very large (2350 seats) and is the home of the English National Opera. Opulent and inviting, this theatre is the place to see not only ENO but visiting opera and ballet companies. Lily Langtry and the famous Ballet Russe performed on this stage.

OPERA HOLLAND PARK   **C3 34**
Holland Park, W8.   ☎ *7602 7856*
During the summer months you can see Opera and Ballet with a good standard of production performed under a large canopy in Holland Park. Previous productions include *Tosca* and *Eugene Onegin*.

ROYAL OPERA HOUSE   **F4 31**
Covent Garden, WC2.   ☎ *7304 4000*
Preceeded by two other theatres, both destroyed by fire, this one dates from 1858 and is not only the home of the Royal Opera, but also the Royal Ballet. Situated in an attractive location it is now adjoined at the side to the small Linbury Studio Theatre and is much more accessible than it used to be. If you anticipate seeing a production I recommend the ballet, it is usually cheaper and the theatre is a lovely experience.

SADLERS WELLS   **B4 24**
Rosebery Avenue, EC1   ☎ *7863 8000*
Eclectic in its dance, opera and lyric programming, Sadlers Wells was never only accessible to the elite; the drawbacks were a small, sloping stage and a vestibule that was almost on the pavement. Now we have London's first new theatre of the 21st century; a great improvement, and a place to see the very best in international arts. Even the walls and ceiling surfaces can become an extension of the scenery and imagery on the stage.

Ticket Agencies

TKTS Booth   **D5 30**
Half Price Tickets with a small service charge are available for same day London West End productions from the booth situated on the south side of Leicester Square by the gardens. Open Monday to Saturday. *Matinees 12.00 - 14.00, Evening 14.00 - 18.30.*

FIRST CALL   ☎ *0870 840 1111*
24 Hour Credit Card Booking for London theatres, some cinemas, and South Bank Concerts etc.

GLOBALTICKETS   ☎ *7734 4555*
Situated in the British Travel Centre in Lower Regent's Street, tickets can be booked not only for the West End but for venues throughout the world.

TICKETMASTER   ☎ *7344 4444*
Credit Card Booking for London shows, sports events, concerts etc.   24 Hour Booking.

Theatres

West End theatre is Shaftesbury Avenue; this is Theatreland. However, it spreads much wider now with the Barbican Centre and the South Bank contributing to the scene. London has only one rival in the world - Broadway. Here are a few theatres that I like and which might be of interest to you for their productions, architecture or decor.

ALMEIDA   **B1 24**
Almeida Street, N1.   ☎ 7359 4404
Situated in Islington, stars come here to act in its productions. Completely refurbished in 2003. Pinter plays have been premiered here.

AMBASSADORS   **D4 30**
West Street, WC2.   ☎ 7836 1171
Agatha Christie's *The Mousetrap* has played here since 1952 - what more can you say!

APOLLO VICTORIA   **A5 38**
Wilton Road, SW1.   ☎ 7630 6262
A large theatre and foyer built as a cinema in the 1930's. The theatre still retains its original almost subterranean decor, although the colouring which was blue and green has been altered.

BARBICAN   **E1 33**
Barbican Centre, EC2.   ☎ 7638 8891
The Royal Shakespeare Company live here as well as in Stratford. Although it has a large capacity all the seats are close to the stage. The Barbican Centre is also worth exploring.

HAYMARKET   **D6 30**
Haymarket,SW1.   ☎ 7930 8800
An 1831 theatre designed by John Nash. An ornate auditorium that saw the premieres of a number of Oscar Wilde plays.

HER MAJESTY'S   **D6 30**
Haymarket, SW1.   ☎ 7494 5400
Opened in 1897, the theatre had great success when it introduced Bernard Shaw's *Pygmalion*. In more recent times it staged the National's *Amadeus* and Andrew Lloyd Webber's *Phantom of the Opera.*

ROYAL NATIONAL THEATRE   **H6 31**
South Bank, SE1.   ☎ 7928 2252
Comprising of three theatres, the Olivier, Lyttelton and Cottesloe (in order of size). The buildings here with the Hayward Gallery always give me the feeling that Kruschev and Brezhnev are going to appear on the balcony. However, it is what is inside that counts and the productions are excellent. The buildings are spacious and comfortable inside.

OPEN AIR THEATRE   **F4 21**
Regent's Park, Inner Circle, NW1.   ☎ 7486 2431
One of the joys of summer are my annual visits to this theatre. Alfresco it is, so take an umbrella and something for a chilly evening. If you have never seen *A Midsummer Nights Dream* this is the perfect place - it is magical. Good buffet food underneath the amphitheatre and you can bring your own wine.

LONDON PALLADIUM   **B4 30**
Argyll Street W1.   ☎ 7494 5020
Designed as a music hall in 1910. The top names have all played here: Judy Garland, Danny Kaye, Frank Sinatra and Irving Berlin with his *This Is The Army* show. The ticket office wall is lined with posters demonstrating the fact that this was, and is, the mecca of light entertainment.

THEATRE ROYAL DRURY LANE   **F4 31**
Catherine Street, SW1.   ☎ 7494 5000
Two other theatres have stood on this site since the time of Charles II. This one dates from 1812 and is the largest theatre in London. Over the years many musical productions - *Oklahoma, Carousel, My Fair Lady, and Miss Saigon* - have been staged here.

Cinemas

Most of London's cinemas have lost their glamour The demand for choice has divided up the buildings so unless they were purpose built, the great decors appear to have gone. Here are some where you might care to see a good film.

CURZON MAYFAIR   **G1 37**
Curzon Street, W1.   ☎ 7369 1720
Real armchair comfort in the heart of Mayfair with programs featuring foreign and art films.

EMPIRE   **H5 22**
Leicester Square, WC2.   ☎ 0870 010 2030
Empirer One is a good place to see a wide screen epic. My parents first date was in this cinema; if I tell you that the star was Lew Ayres, guess the film.

NATIONAL FILM THEATRE   **G6 31**
South Bank, SE1.   ☎ 7928 3232
Underneath Waterloo bridge, this is a repertory cinema, changing daily and showing great films and classics - Eisenstein through to Tarentino.

ODEON   **D5 30**
Leicester Square WC2.   ☎ 0870 505 0007
The largest ordinary screen and cinema in the metropolis. It is used for premieres, when celebrities bring panache to the occasions.

BFI LONDON IMAX   **H1 39**
Waterloo Rd. SE1.   ☎ 7902 1234
The largest screen in Great Britain, the place for a cinematic experience, rather than the latest film.

Jazz in London

Jazz in London is thriving. Some older clubs are still around, and thanks to the Pizza Express chain policy of providing jazz in their restaurants, venues have increased. Ronnie Scott's (D4 30) does not need an introduction: the perfect club, if only the clientele were real jazz fans. My memories apart from the late Ronnie Scott's jokes include standing next to Jane Russell in the vestibule: she had come to hear her friend, Anita O'Day (the lady with the hat in the film, *Jazz on a Summers Day)*. Another extremely poignant memory was seeing Bill Evans two weeks before he died. Ronnie's also has a separate Latin club - Club Latino - one of the best in London's thriving salsa scene. The Pizza Express in Dean Street (C3 30) and the one at Hyde Park Corner (F3 37) both offer a menu of mainstream jazz and are highly highly recommended. The 100 Club (C3 30) in Oxford Street has been going so long it is amazing. The traditional, blues and dixieland music are accompanied here by Chinese food. Reasonable admission charges.
I like the 606 Club (H6 43) in Chelsea; gourmet food, good modern jazz and it opens for seven days a week. The Jazz Cafe (D6 19) in a former bank building in Camden Town, offers the best in modern music and jazz and attracts some great musicians like Bobby Watson, José Feliciano. Often over the Christmas period, the place gently rocks to the music of the London Community Gospel Choir.

> **THE BULL'S HEAD** On the southside of the river Thames near Barnes Bridge in Lonsdale Road, this pub has served jazz with excellent beer every day for many years. All the best musicians love the place; the audience is usually appreciative, and the music eclectic. Get a train from Waterloo to Barnes Bridge Station and walk about 30 yards, or go by the tube to Hammersmith and catch a 209 bus in the terminal to Barnes Bridge.

DOCKLANDS

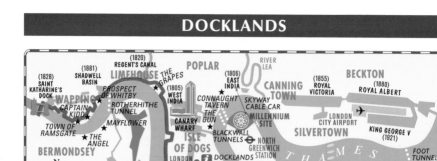

Map of Docklands showing:

(1820) REGENT'S CANAL · POPLAR · RIVER LEA · (1806) EAST INDIA · (1855) ROYAL VICTORIA · BECKTON · (1880) ROYAL ALBERT · (1828) SAINT KATHARINE'S DOCK · (1881) SHADWELL BASIN · LIMEHOUSE · THE GRAPES · PROSPECT OF WHITBY · (1805) WEST INDIA · CONNAUGHT TAVERN · CANNING TOWN · SKYWAY CABLE CAR · WAPPING · CAPTAIN KIDD · ROTHERHITHE TUNNEL · THE GUN · MILLENNIUM SITE · LONDON CITY AIRPORT · KING GEORGE V (1921) · TOWN OF RAMSGATE · MAYFLOWER · CANARY WHARF · BLACKWALL TUNNELS · NORTH GREENWICH · SILVERTOWN · THE ANGEL · BERMONDSEY · N · ISLE OF DOGS · LONDON ARENA · DOCKLANDS VISITORS CENTRE · THAMES · FOOT TUNNEL · CANADA WATER · MILLWALL (1862) · WATERMANS ARMS · THAMES FLOOD BARRIER · WOOLWICH · DEPTFORD ROYAL SHIPYARD ESTABLISHED IN 1515 · ISLAND GARDENS · FROM ISLAND GARDENS THERE IS AN INCOMPARABLE VIEW OF GREENWICH · THE THAMES PATH · FOLLOW THE ACORN SYMBOL · FOOT TUNNEL · GREENWICH · Scale of Miles 0 1 2 · Kilometres 0 1 3

★ HISTORIC OR INTERESTING PUBLIC HOUSES

The Canary Wharf Tower with its pyramid top, fifty storeys, exterior of stainless steel and height of 800 feet dominates London's skyline: its red flashing light tells you that this is Docklands. The architect is Cesar Pelli, whose other major achievement was the tragic twin towered World Trade Center in New York. The tower is the apex and the centre of the regeneration area on the Isle of Dogs, which now harbours some of the finest modern architecture and planning to be seen in London. The best way to reach the area is by the Docklands Light Railway, which takes you directly to Canary Wharf. At this moment in time it is no Manhattan; it is a daytime, working place, where most of the national newspapers have taken roots (in spite of massive opposition from their work forces). For evening pleasures and other activities you have to go up river, but they are working on it.

THE DOCKS The docks, or the old Port of London used to begin to the east of Tower Bridge, and they stretched down river to North Woolwich. Although their history goes back a long time. It was 1515 when an important phase began; Henry VIII established the Royal Shipyards at Deptford and Woolwich. Wide-spread expansion followed during Queen Elizabeth I's reign, which heralded the rise of London as the world's leading financial centre. The growth of empire, steam-engines and industry of the Victorian era created the need for the new deep water docks, and the warehouses which were built to accomodate the huge increase of commerce in the area. The construction site at that time was the biggest ever known. In 1940 Hitler tried to annihilate the docklands. He did not succeed, although he caused great damage: some of the old sugar warehouses burned for many days.

DOCKLANDS LIGHT RAILWAY
- TOWER GATEWAY
- SHADWELL
- LIMEHOUSE
- WESTFERRY
- WEST INDIA DOCK
- CANARY WHARF
- HERON QUAYS
- SOUTH QUAY
- CROSSHARBOUR LONDON ARENA
- MUDCHUTE
- ISLAND GARDENS

BORN AGAIN

The end of the docks came in the 1970's with the advent of new technology: containers, mechanical handling, and roll on/off terminals, did away with the majority of dockers. Today, the area is more middle class as city workers move into the renovated iron and brick warehouses. They have their own computer controlled driverless overhead railway, the Docklands Light, and North Greenwich underground station - the largest in Europe - which connects with central London. The 12,500 seated London Arena holds boxing and wrestling and large pop concerts.

RIVERSIDE PUBLIC HOUSES

There are quite a few pubs in the docklands area that still retain some of the original atmosphere, and here are a few to whet your whistle.

TOWN OF RAMSGATE 62 Wapping High St. E1. A dimly lit pub where the *Hanging Judge* Jefferies finally got his due. The cellars were dungeons where convicts were kept prior to deportation to Australia.
CAPTAIN KIDD 108 Wapping High St. E1. Not an old pub, but you would never know. Close by the police station and with a restaurant.
PROSPECT OF WHITBY, 57 Wapping Wall, E1. The oldest of all the riverside London pubs dating from 1520. Samuel Pepys and Dickens drank here.
THE GRAPES, 76 Narrow Street, E14. With a river overhang, Dickens affiliations and a cosy small restaurant, renowned for its fresh fish.
THE GUN, 27 Cold Harbour, E14. Across from the millennium dome, near the entrance to West India dock, it is alleged to be the place where Nelson brought Lady Hamilton; he lived nearby.
THE MAYFLOWER, 117 Rotherhithe St, SE16. The Pilgrim Fathers ship was moored here and the ship's captain is buried across the street in St.Mary's.
THE ANGEL, 101 Bermondsey Wall East, SE16. Parts of this pub are very ancient indeed. It also has very good views up river to Tower Bridge.

THE MILLENNIUM DOME

Built to protect exhibition pavilions from the elements for the year-long show, this massive big top was built to last much longer than the celebrations. Designed by Richard Rogers, it is the same height as Nelson's Column and could encompass thirteen Albert Halls or two Wembley Stadiums, It is now used for occasional concerts, etc!

INDEX TO STREETS

ABBREVIATIONS   *The letters following a name indicate the Square and Page Number*

App. - Approach	E. - East	Lit. - Little	Sth. - South
Arc. - Arcade	Emb. - Embankment	Lr. - Lower	Sq. - Square
Av. - Avenue	Est. - Estate	Ms. - Mews	Sta. - Station
Bri. - Bridge	Flds. - Fields	Mt. - Mount	St. - Street
Blds. - Buildings	Gdns.- Gardens	Nth. - North	Ter. - Terrace
Cir. - Circus	Gte. - Gate	Pal. - Palace	Up. - Upper
Clo. - Close	Gt. - Great	Pde. - Parade	Vw. - View
Cotts.- Cottages	Grn. - Green	Pk. - Park	Vs. - Villas
Ct. - Court	Gro. - Grove	Pass.- Passage	Wk. - Walk
Cres. - Crescent	Ho. - House	Pl. - Place	W. - West
Dri. - Drive	La. - Lane	Rd. - Road	Yd. - Yard

PRINCESS DIANA MEMORIAL FOUNTAIN   B2 36

HAMPSTEAD AND HIGHGATE INDEX
PAGES 50 - 51

Every effort has been made throughout this Mapguide to ensure that the information given is accurate, while the Publishers would be grateful to learn of errors, they can not accept responsibility for any loss or expense caused by any errors or updating which may have occurred.

I would like to thank British Waterways for permission to use their photograph of Snowdon's Aviary on page 49,
and English Heritage for the Page 5 reproduction of 'Old London Bridge' by Claude de Jongh.
The front cover and page I illustrations were by Ronald Maddox PRI, FCSD.
The back cover photograph of the 'Wellington Arch and War Memorial' by Michael Middleditch
Page 8 Bobby Charlton illustration by permission of the National Portrait Gallery,London
Globe theatre photograph by Richard Kalina permission of Shakespeare's Globe.
Inside Cover 'Balloon View of London' by permission of the British Library
30 St. Mary Axe on page 33 reproduced by permission of Swiss Re.

MAPGUIDES & MAPS BY MICHAEL MIDDLEDITCH
PUBLISHED BY PENGUIN BOOKS

The PARIS MAPGUIDE   ISBN 0-14-14-6904-8
A 64 page double award winning publication. Clear and colourful, containing a wealth of information including an original Metro map: easy to read and ideal to carry with you. Features on the Louvre, Versailles etc.

The AMSTERDAM MAPGUIDE   ISBN 0-14-028452-4
A unique and colourful publication to this interesting and stimulating city. An ideal companion to take with you on your walks or canal cruise for that long weekend trip.

The NEW YORK MAPGUIDE   ISBN 0-14-029459-7
The indispensable guide to Manhattan, containing maps, entertainments, walks, a guide to the great 20th century architecture, as well as detailed plans of the Bronx Zoo, the Botanical Gardens and Prospect Park, Brooklyn.

The Penguin Map of THE WORLD   ISBN 0-14-051528-3
A clear, colourful map featuring Flags of the World, crammed with information on an unusual projection. Ideal as a wall map for office or home.

The Penguin Map of EUROPE   ISBN 0-14-051286-1
For the family, schools, and offices: includes the Urals, all of Turkey and parts of Algeria, Morocco, Tunisia, Iraq and Iran: National flags and Currency details.

The Penguin Map of the BRITISH ISLES   ISBN 0-14-046993-1
Ideal for route planning, all of the Counties are named and indicated in colour: includes part of Normandy. Useful for business or pleasure.

The Penguin Map of NORTH AMERICA   ISBN 0-14-051186-5
Includes Hawaii, Iceland, Central America and the Western Caribbean: New England inset at enlarged scale: National Parks and National Flags.

The ST ALBANS MAPGUIDE   ISBN 0-9513390-1-X
Published by MICHAEL GRAHAM PUBLICATIONS, This is the author's home town; it contains an ancient abbey, and the remains of Verulamium the Roman town.
The MAPGUIDE won a British Cartographic Society award.

PENGUIN BOOKS

New Format First Published 2000
7 8 9 10

Published by the Penguin Group
Penguin Books Ltd, 80 Strand, London WC2R 0RL, England
Penguin Putnam Inc., 375 Hudson Street, New York, New York 10014, USA
Penguin Books Australia Ltd, 250 Camberwell Road, Camberwell, Victoria 3124, Australia
Penguin Books Canada Ltd, 10 Alcorn Avenue, Toronto, Ontario, Canada M4V 3B2
Penguin Books India (P) Ltd, 11 Community Centre, Panchsheel Park, New Delhi - 110 017, India
Penguin Books (NZ) Ltd, Cnr. Rosedale and Airborne Roads, Albany, Auckland, New Zealand
Penguin Books (South Africa) (Pty) Ltd, 24 Sturdee Avenue, Rosebank 2196, South Africa

Penguin Books Ltd, Registered Offices: 80 Strand, London WC2R 0RL, England